LEARNING ABOUT
Liturgy
Catechesis
For Children
And Their Families

Dorothy Kosinski Carola

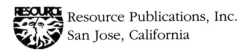
Resource Publications, Inc.
San Jose, California

Reprint Department
Resource Publications, Inc.
160 E. Virginia Street #290
San Jose, CA 95112-5876
1-408-286-8505 voice
1-408-287-8748 fax

ISBN 0-89390-497-X

Printed in the United States of America

01 02 03 04 05 | 5 4 3 2 1

Editorial director: Nick Wagner
Production coordinator: Mike Sagara
Copyeditor: Robin Witkin

Original artwork by Sr. Kathleen Vasselli, SSND

The author gratefully acknowledges the invaluable assistance of Msgr. William J. Koplik. His wisdom and vision, his gifts of time, talent, and inspiration, contributed immensely to both the content of this book and to the process by which it became a reality.

The author is also grateful for the assistance of her husband, Hugh M. Carola, and her sister, Katherine M. Schacht.

For Bill

Contents

Part 1: Master Copies of Lesson Handouts

Part 2: Lesson Plans

How to Use this Book

Learning about Liturgy is intended to open up the treasures of liturgical spirituality to children and their families. It provides both catechesis *for* liturgy and catechesis *from* liturgy. Catechesis *for* liturgy means that participants will be better prepared to fruitfully celebrate Mass. Catechesis *from* liturgy means that the Mass itself becomes our "textbook." We will look to the Scriptures, prayers, gestures, and symbols of our liturgy to discover the heart of the Christian message. Participants will become more conscious of the role of liturgy in Christian formation and more familiar with the components of the ritual. They will begin to appropriate the spirituality that informs and enlivens the liturgy.

The Intended Audience for *Learning about Liturgy*

Learning about Liturgy was prepared for use with middle-grade children (those in grades four through six). Used in a family setting, or in a class of mixed ages, the program can certainly appeal to and benefit older children as well, perhaps through age fourteen.

Possible Ways to Use *Learning about Liturgy*

Learning about Liturgy is designed to be very flexible. It can be used in a wide variety of settings. Consider some of these possibilities:

- as a resource for home use for parents who want to be more active in their child(ren)'s spiritual formation.

- as the principal content of a classroom-based parish catechetical program.

- as a supplement to any parish or parochial school catechetical program. Any or all of the handouts can be incorporated into any text-based or lectionary-based program.

- as family-centered catechesis, incorporating a variety of age levels.

- as a home-based program, for use by individual families or clusters of families. It is ideal for families who cannot participate in the regular parish catechetical program, and for families who wish to supplement the parish program at home. It is also an ideal choice for smaller or rural parishes that do not have extensive parish-based programs.

- as a way to enrich the catechetical and liturgical experience of children's choirs.

- as part of the formation and training of altar servers.

- as a component of the catechumenal process with children of catechetical age.
- as an independent four-week unit inserted into the parochial school's standard religion curriculum.
- as a Religion Learning Center in a parochial school classroom.
- as Vacation Church School curriculum.
- as a curriculum resource for Catholic families who home-school their children.

How to Schedule The Lessons

The most effective way of proceeding through these lessons is the obvious one: Begin with Lesson 1 and continue through Lesson 17, in sequence.

However, if used as a supplement to an existing catechetical program, time constraints may not allow you to include all seventeen lessons. The best suggestion for these circumstances is to use Lessons 1, 2, 3, 4, 10, 14, 16, and 17. Lessons 1 and 2 put the children in touch with the role of liturgy in the lives of Catholics, and provide an overview of liturgy in general. Lessons 3 and 16 deal with the Introductory Rites and Concluding Rite, while Lessons 4 and 10 provide an overview (only) of the Liturgy of the Word and the Liturgy of the Eucharist. Lesson 14 looks at the Real Presence of Christ in the Eucharist, a topic always in need of review. Lesson 17, dealing with Sunday celebrations in the absence of a priest, may not seem essential, but all Catholics need help in facing and shaping our future as a church. In this way, a more detailed handling of the Liturgy of the Word and the Liturgy of the Eucharist will be missing, but the fundamentals will have been covered.

Using the After-Mass Worksheet

In the Appendix, you will find an After-Mass Worksheet. It is intended to help children (and adults) reflect on their experience of worship. In every lesson plan, the After-Mass Worksheet is listed as an optional assignment. It is listed there as a reminder to the catechist to consider this option now and again, not to indicate that it ought to be part of every lesson. It is up to each catechist to determine if, how, and when to request that the group complete the worksheet. Here are some possibilities:

- Expecting the entire worksheet to be completed every week could easily become tedious, making liturgy more of a chore than a prayer and a joy. Instead, consider requesting only one section of the worksheet to be completed in a given week, so that the entire worksheet is completed over the course of five weeks.
- You might request the completion of the entire worksheet only once per liturgical season.
- Families might use the worksheet to start discussion at home, without actually writing their responses.

Tips for the Parish Catechetical Leader

- If you have a number of families or catechists using this program at once, you can make your job and theirs much easier by previewing the In Our Parish sections of the lessons. Make a list of the information group leaders will need. Consider providing this information in a monthly or seasonal newsletter, at occasional group leader meetings, as a feature in the parish bulletin, or in some other way that makes sense in your setting. This will prevent you from having several families or catechists requesting information from you independently of one another.

- Consider providing a folder or binder in which the children can keep their handouts. Encouraging them to keep all their handouts together lets them know how much you value this endeavor and will allow them to see the "big picture" accumulate piece by piece.

- If you are supervising a number of families who are using *Learning about Liturgy* in their own homes, the suggestion that various parish ministers be invited to speak to the group may not be practical, especially if these ministers were to receive a dozen or more invitations at once. Consider providing a brief session with the minister in question for *all* the families after a particular Mass each week, or as needed. Keep the ministers apprised of the schedule and of the questions or topic they will be expected to address.

- For a truly complete approach to liturgy, consider integrating the lessons from the companion volume *Learning about the Liturgical Seasons,* also available from Resource Publications, Inc. It contains handouts and lesson plans for each of the church's liturgical seasons, using the same approach found in this book.

Tips for All Catechists

- You may wish to reproduce *your* copy of the handout on 8½-by-14-inch paper. This will allow room for you to make your own notes and teaching suggestions directly under the text.

- If possible, provide a folder or binder in which the children can keep their handouts. Encouraging them to keep all their handouts together lets them know how much you value this endeavor and will allow them to see the "big picture" accumulate piece by piece.

- If you are using *Learning about Liturgy* in a group composed entirely of children, you may wish to make a habit of assigning the Living Our Liturgy and/or Something to Do sections as work to be completed at home. This will bring the ideas covered in class home to the children's families. If you choose this option, remember to begin each session with a review of what the children did at home.

- The lesson plans include many suggestions for the use of music. If you are tempted to ignore these because you believe you cannot sing, have several people confirm for you that you are absolutely tone-deaf before you give up. As long as you can carry a tune, you can help your group sing. In the unlikely event that you really can't sing, consider finding a member of your group who can lead the singing when necessary. Some advanced planning will ensure that this individual is prepared when needed. If that is not an option, recordings of many of the pieces are available. Your parish music director may be able to help.

- Unless you are closely involved in liturgical preparation in your parish, you will probably need the assistance of other parish personnel at various points throughout the program, and specifically in addressing the In Our Parish section of each lesson. Forge good relationships with them, but do not make a nuisance of yourself. Early planning is the key. Look ahead to know what information you will need. Allow the people whose assistance you require enough time to gather the information and get back to you. You may have a less-than-delightful experience if you make a habit of needing information or assistance "today."

- Learn from your parish catechetical leader whether the companion volume to this program, *Learning about the Liturgical Seasons*, is available for your use. It contains handouts and lessons plans for each of the church's liturgical seasons. You may wish to integrate these with the *Learning about Liturgy* lessons for a more thorough treatment of what we experience when we participate in the liturgy every week.

Tips for Parent-Catechists

- Set aside a specific time each week to use *Learning about Liturgy* with your family. Set aside time for yourself to prepare in advance.

- This program avoids using words like "class," "classroom," and "teacher," specifically because we had you in mind. Nonetheless, some aspects of the lesson plans will seem geared to classroom-based catechetical programs. This will be most apparent in two ways:

  1. The lesson plans assume that the catechist is not well acquainted with every member of the group. Because you are certainly well acquainted with your own children, you can easily make the adjustments. For example, the lesson plan may say: "Discover whether anyone in your group knows someone who serves as a lector or communion minister." As a parent, you already have this information. So you might say something like "Remember how excited you were to see Uncle Joseph ministering communion?" or "Mom was really nervous the first time she proclaimed the Scriptures at Mass, wasn't she?"

  2. The suggestion that various parish minsters be invited to visit your group may seem better suited to a classroom situation. Nonetheless, you and your children could speak informally with such people after Mass with much the same benefit. Check to learn whether your parish might provide a brief session with these ministers for all the families using the program.

- If possible, provide a folder or binder in which your child(ren) can keep their handouts. Encouraging them to keep all their handouts together lets them know how much you value this endeavor and will allow them to see the "big picture" accumulate piece by piece.

Part 1

Master Copies Of Lesson Handouts

LEARNING ABOUT
Liturgy

Lesson 1 Handout

What Is Liturgy? #1

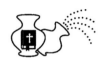

Our Lives

Alyssa and Cassie were fascinated as they watched the potter working at her wheel. The lump of wet clay seemed to turn into a lovely vase as if by magic. But it wasn't really magic. It was the constant turning of the wheel and the skilled, experienced, loving hands of the potter. She knew exactly how to place her hands around the clay. She could shape it just the way she wanted. If it didn't look right to her, she could start over. If the clay wasn't centered and it flew off the wheel, she could put it back together. Her studio was filled with many kinds of clay creations—bowls, cups, plates, and vases. Each one was unique and each one was beautiful.

Have you ever seen a potter at work? A potter is someone who makes things out of clay by turning the clay on a pottery wheel. The potter carefully centers the clay on the wheel. As the wheel turns around and around, the potter shapes and molds the clay. The potter turns each lump of clay into something beautiful and useful.

Our Liturgy

The prophet Jeremiah tells us that God is like a potter, and we are like the potter's clay. God is always active in our lives, shaping us into God's people. God's skilled, loving hands are molding the clay of our lives, forming us into beautiful and useful vessels.

For Catholics, the eucharistic liturgy (Mass) is the most important way God is active in our lives. By regularly attending Mass, God shapes and forms us into the church. Week after week, we come to

"Just like the clay in the potter's hand, so are you in my hand, O house of Israel."

—Jer 18:6

be shaped by the Potter God. The liturgy, then, is like God's pottery wheel. It is the tool God uses to help form us as God's people.

At Mass, we hear the Scriptures—the stories of how God saves us. We hear Jesus tell us that the kingdom of God has already begun, and that we can live it now. We pray and sing. We remember Jesus' saving death on the cross and his resurrection from the dead. We receive the Body and Blood of Christ in the Eucharist. In all these ways, God is molding us. God is forming us. God is shaping us. We are becoming beautiful earthen vessels; we are becoming kingdom people!

Something to Know

Liturgy is the public prayer of the church. The eucharistic liturgy is also called "Mass." The word "Mass" comes from "dismissal," which means "going forth."

Living Our Liturgy

A lump of clay gets dry and hard if it is left out too long. The same thing can happen to us when we leave ourselves out of Mass. Spiritually, we dry out. It can be much harder for the Potter God to mold us! We need to be at Mass every week so that our faith stays fresh. That way, we continue to become the kingdom people God wants us to be.

When we let God mold and shape us, we can live God's way better the rest of the week.

Something to Do

In this space, write a letter to a friend explaining why it would be a good idea to go to Mass this weekend.

_____

_____

_____

_____

_____

_____

In this space, list three things you do to live the way God wants you to live. (*Hint:* Do this without naming any "church-y" things like prayers, CCD, communion, going to Mass.)

_____

_____

_____

_____

_____

_____

_____

_____

_____

_____

_____

_____

_____

_____

_____

This handout taken from
Learning about Liturgy,
© 2001 Dorothy Kosinski Carola.

LEARNING ABOUT
Liturgy

What Is Liturgy? #2

Our Lives

Alyssa and Cassie had just enough money to buy one of the prettiest vases in the potter's shop. It would be their grandmother's birthday present.

Grandma was delighted when she saw the handmade vase. Right away, she put it on display on the shelf in the living room. "But, Grandma," Alyssa urged, "a vase is supposed to have something in it. You can't just leave it empty." "True enough," Grandma agreed. So she took some cuttings from her favorite plant, filled the vase with water, and placed the cuttings in the vase. "These cuttings will grow roots and I'll be able to plant them. Maybe each of you would like to have one of the plants when they grow." Alyssa and Cassie thought that was a great way for Grandma to use the new vase.

Our Liturgy

"All the activity of the Church leads us to liturgy. At the same time, the liturgy is the fountain from which all the strength and grace of the Church flows" (an adaptation of the *Constitution on the Sacred Liturgy* 10).

Like Grandma's new vase, the earthen vessels God is shaping us into are not meant to stay empty either. They are meant to be filled with the life of Jesus.

The opening passage is from the *Constitution on the Sacred Liturgy*. It shows us another way to think about liturgy. It says that our eucharistic liturgy is like a great fountain. Each week, we come to the fountain so that we can be filled with God's grace.

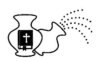

"The light of God has shown in our hearts. We are filled with the glory of Jesus Christ. But we have this treasure in clay jars, so everyone will know that this power belongs to God and does not come from us."

—adapted from 2 Cor 4:6–7

Grace is the life of Jesus in our hearts. God gives us the grace of Jesus through the Holy Spirit. Grace is like water, always flowing freely. God is pouring it out for us all the time, especially at liturgy. When our own clay jar is filled with the life of Jesus, other people will be able to see Jesus in us. They will know that the good things we do come from God. We will not be empty. We will be filled with Jesus.

Something to Know

Our eucharistic liturgy has four main parts:

- **The Introductory Rites**
- **The Liturgy of the Word**
- **The Liturgy of the Eucharist**
- **The Concluding Rite**

Living Our Liturgy

When we are filled with Jesus, people see God's light shining in us. God's grace can pour out of us and into the lives of others. When we are kind and helpful, when we show concern for other people, God will be helping them through us. Perhaps Jesus isn't really forming us into vases. Perhaps he is forming us into pitchers and sieves, so that his grace can flow through us, and pour out of us, into the lives of others.

Who needs to see Jesus in you? There might be someone at home or in school or in your neighborhood. There might be someone farther away. How will you share with them the life of Jesus in you?

Something to Do

When you are at Mass this week, see if you can tell when each of these parts begins. Write your answers here:

The Introductory Rites begin with _____

_____

_____

The Liturgy of the Word begins with_____

_____

_____

This handout taken from
Learning about Liturgy,
© 2001 Dorothy Kosinski Carola.
All rights reserved.

The Liturgy of the Eucharist begins with _____

_____

_____

_____

The Concluding Rite begins with _____

_____

_____

_____

Notes

LEARNING ABOUT
Liturgy

Lesson 3 Handout

Introductory Rites

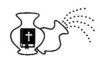

Our Lives

The preparations were almost finished. Kelly and Ashley's bedroom was tidy, even under the bed. In fact, Mom and Dad had been cleaning the apartment for several days. Everyone was excited about the family reunion this weekend. They had already bought lots of fancy paper plates and started preparing some special foods. Getting ready took some extra work, but this was going to be a very special gathering.

Our Liturgy

Our gathering on Sunday is also very special. Each week, God's people get together to be with one another and to celebrate all that God has done for them in Jesus.

Before we can participate in this special gathering, we need to get ready. We need to prepare ourselves to experience Jesus in word and sacrament.

Some of the getting ready happens before we arrive at the church. We prepare as individuals or as a family. Perhaps you will read the Scriptures for the Mass at home. Perhaps you will spend some quiet time in prayer. The time before and after Mass should be a time of calm and relaxation. As much as we can, we try to keep Sunday as a day of rest. Those who go to Mass on Saturday evening start their day of rest even earlier!

The church has another way of helping us get ready. Everyone who will receive the Eucharist is expected to fast one hour in advance. That means we eat nothing for one hour before Mass. This helps us focus on the most important food we are about to eat—the Body and Blood of Jesus. Fasting helps us to be hungry for God.

While you are at home getting ready, many other parishioners are doing the same thing in their homes. As everyone heads toward the

"Prepare the way of the Lord."

—**Mark 1:3**

church, it's like the entrance procession has already begun! The church—the People of God—is gathering.

When you arrive at the church, there may be people there who help you get ready. Greeters or Ministers of Hospitality may welcome you as you arrive. They may welcome newcomers and assist the elderly or the handicapped. People may greet and speak with each other. Everyone who comes to celebrate the Eucharist should feel at home. What helps you feel at home in your church? How do you help others feel at home?

Some of the ways we prepare for liturgy are built into the Mass. These are called the Introductory Rites. All the getting ready and the gathering we have been doing so far comes together in the Introductory Rites. When it's time to begin, everyone sings and the entrance procession begins. The priest and other ministers join in the procession. The singing of the entrance song is an important moment of getting ready. Now we are no longer getting ready as individuals. We are getting ready as a community. We are gathering as one body. Singing is a great way for people to be united. When we raise our voices in song, we are one. We are becoming a worshiping community.

After the sign of the cross, the priest greets us with these words: "The grace and peace of God our Father and the Lord Jesus Christ be with you." We answer: *And also with you.*" (See Introductory Rites, Greeting, in the sacramentary.)

Next comes the Penitential Rite. During the Penitential Rite, we remember that we are sinners. We remember how baptized people should live, and we praise Jesus for being so merciful to us.

The Penitential Rite can take different forms. On some Sundays, especially during the Easter season, the priest might sprinkle everyone with holy water to remind us of our baptism. At other times, we might say the "I confess" prayer. Another form of the Penitential Rite proclaims Jesus' mercy. We say, "Lord, have mercy. Christ, have mercy. Lord, have mercy," after each invocation.

The Penitential Rite might be spoken or sung. No matter which form we use, the Penitential Rite helps us get ready to hear God's word by reminding us how much we need God.

Following the Penitential Rite, we say or sing the "Glory to God." This is a joyous prayer of praise to God and to Jesus. After the "Glory to God," the priest asks us to pray. There will be some silence while everyone prays quietly. Then the priest collects all our prayers into one by saying the Opening Prayer. The Opening Prayer is different each week. It is always a prayer that we will be open to Jesus and become more like him.

Now we are ready. We have gathered. We have become a worshiping community. Our hearts are open to hear God's word and to remember Jesus' saving death.

Something to Know

The Introductory Rites are:

- **The Entrance Song**
- **The Greeting** — which includes the sign of the cross.
- **The Penitential Rite**
- **Glory to God** — except during Advent and Lent.
- **The Opening Prayer**

 ## Living Our Liturgy

When we prepare well for the liturgy, we will be ready to listen to God. We will be united as a community of faith. Take that with you when you leave Mass, and Christian living will be much easier for you. Stay ready to listen to God, and stay close to God's people.

Something To Do

List one way you will prepare for liturgy this week.

_____

_____

Describe how Sunday is different from the other days in your house. Is it a "family day"? Is there a special dinner? Is there time to relax? Do you go visiting or have company? Tell about anything that sets Sunday apart from the other days. Plan a way to make next Sunday special.

_____

_____

_____

_____

_____

This handout taken from
Learning about Liturgy,
© 2001 Dorothy Kosinski Carola.
All rights reserved.

In Our Parish

- Who are the people who welcome you and help you feel at home when you come to church? Learn their names.

- What do people do to help others feel welcome?

- Who is in the entrance procession?

- What form of the penitential rite is used most often?

- Is the "Glory to God" sung or spoken? Is it sung at some times and spoken at others?

Notes

LEARNING ABOUT
Liturgy

Liturgy of the Word: Overview

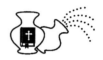

"Let anyone with ears listen."

—Matt 13:9

Our Lives

Marc wasn't so sure he would like his new school. He already missed his friends from his old school, and he was worried about being the new kid. What if he couldn't find his classroom? What if nobody sat with him at lunch? What if his new class was ahead of him in math?

Marc didn't want to worry all by himself for the whole weekend, so he called Jamal, his best friend from his old neighborhood. Marc could hear loud music in his friend's room, and other kids were there laughing and having a good time. Marc began to talk about his worries, but his friend suddenly asked, "Did you hear the new song by Chopped Liver? Joey just brought over their new CD. You should hear it; it's awesome!" Jamal turned the music up louder so Marc could hear it, but Marc wasn't interested. "I'll call you back another time," Marc shouted into the phone, then hung up.

Marc found his father in the basement sorting through boxes. "You know, Dad, I wish I could have visited this new school so I could at least find the right classroom on Monday," Marc started. Dad just about cut him off: "You'll find it just fine. There's nothing to worry about. Now could you hand me that big carton over there? I think that's where I packed the screwdrivers and hammer. You haven't seen my tools, have you? Mom wants me to hang up the curtains in the two bedrooms and the living room." Marc carried the carton to his father and walked away.

Marc found his mom upstairs, ironing curtains. "You know, I won't even know where my classroom is on Monday." Mom stopped ironing and turned toward Marc. "Sounds like you're a little nervous," she said. "Well, a little," Marc continued. Mom pulled the stepstool

19

over and sat down. Marc plopped down on the floor opposite her. He went on about all the things that worried him about the new school. Mom sat quietly and watched his face as he spoke.

When we have something important to talk about, we want someone to listen. You can tell if someone is really listening or not. What are some ways you can tell? What are some ways Marc could tell?

We want our listeners to *respond* to us. They might respond just by paying attention, or by letting us know they understand us. They might give us a hug or promise to help us. But we always need a response to be sure we have been heard.

Our Liturgy

At Mass, listening and responding are the two most important activities in the Liturgy of the Word. God has something important to say to us, and God does this through the Scripture readings.

At liturgy, Jesus is present to us in many ways. He is present to us in the assembly of the people and in the priest. He is present to us in the consecrated bread and wine and in the Scriptures. That is why we say that the proclamation of the word at liturgy is a *living word*. It is the living Lord who is communicating with us.

The most important thing we can do is to *listen*. Not *just* with our ears, but with our hearts. To listen , we sit still. We look at the lector or the priest who is proclaiming God's word. We think about what we have heard.

It is important to realize that our main activity during the Liturgy of the Word is *listening* and NOT *reading*. This is not a classroom, where the "students" read along with the "teacher." This is the assembly of God's people, gathered to hear the proclamation of God's word. Just put your heart and your ears together and you will find out how wonderful God is.

The liturgy lets us *respond* to God's word too. One way is through the periods of quiet that follow the first reading, the second reading, and the homily. During these silences we meditate about the Scriptures we have just heard and imagine how we might respond. Another form of response is the psalm. By singing one of these prayers from Scripture, we take the day's Scriptures into our hearts.

Our posture during the Liturgy of the Word helps us listen. We sit down to listen to the first and second reading, and to sing the psalm. We are relaxed and open. We stand up to listen to the Gospel to show that we are paying *extra* attention to the most important reading.

Something to Know

Here's what we find in the Liturgy of the Word:

- **First Reading** — usually from the Old Testament.

- **Psalm** — which is sung.

- **Second Reading** — from the New Testament, usually the letters.
- **Gospel Acclamation** — which is sung.
- **Gospel reading**
- **Homily**
- **Creed**
- **Prayer of the Faithful** — also known as the Universal Prayer, or General Intercessions; these may also be sung.

 ## Living Our Liturgy

The best way to tell if someone was listening is if he or she does what we asked. This is also the most important response we make to the Word of God, but it doesn't happen at Mass. It happens after Mass, when we *go forth* to live out the Scriptures we have heard.

Something to Do

To help you listen better without reading at Mass, try this:

- Read the day's Scriptures *before* you go to Mass. Then just listen very attentively while you are at Mass. Try this for several weeks. How do you hear God speaking to you in the Scriptures?

_____

_____

_____

_____

_____

_____

- Write down the citations for the Scriptures of the coming Sunday. Review them with your folks before Mass next weekend.

First Reading: _____

Psalm: _____

Second Reading: _____

Gospel: _____

In Our Parish

- Is there a large Bible or Book of the Gospels on display in your church? If so, why do you think it is there?

- Pay attention to the periods of silence in the Liturgy of the Word. Do they seem very long to you, or very short? Ask a priest or a lector how long each period of silence is. Were you surprised with the answer?

_____

Notes

This handout taken from
Learning about Liturgy,
© 2001 Dorothy Kosinski Carola.
All rights reserved.

LEARNING ABOUT
Liturgy

Lesson 5 Handout

Liturgy of the Word: First Reading

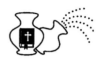

"Indeed, the Word of God is living and active."

—Heb 4:12

Our Lives

Jake was eager for the school day to end, because today was Thursday. That meant that Uncle Hughie would be picking him up from school. Jake loved to hear Uncle Hughie's stories of when he was a boy.

"Tell that story about when you and your friends built that fort in the woods," Jake prodded, as he and Uncle Hughie shared an after-school snack. "Haven't I told that story about eight times now?" Uncle Hughie teased. "No, only three," Jake continued, "but that's the best one. Or maybe the one about when you and Dad tried to get the dog to go trick-or-treating with you so you could get more candy. Maybe that's my favorite." "You can have any story you want as soon as this hot chocolate is ready," Uncle Hughie promised.

Families often treasure the stories that tell their history. You have probably heard the stories about when you were born, or about when you were adopted. Perhaps your family tells stories about when they first came to this country. You might enjoy telling the story of some accomplishment or honor you received, or the story of an important game you won. Some stories mean so much to us that we tell them over and over again. What stories are important to you and your family?

Our Liturgy

God's family has stories that we treasure too. They are the stories of God's salvation, and they are collected in the Bible.

These stories are so important to us as Catholic Christians that we gather every weekend to hear them.

The first reading is usually taken from the Old Testament. That's the part of the Bible that tells about how God saved God's people *before* the coming of Jesus. They are the stories of the Jewish people, who were the first to know God. Beginning with Abraham, God made a covenant with them, promising to be their God and promising that they would be God's special people. The story of how God saved this people over and over, through many, many years and through many, many trials, is told in the Old Testament.

The most important event in God's plan of salvation is the coming of Jesus. Jesus came to complete the salvation God started through the Jewish people. So the stories of the Jewish people are our stories too. That's why the first reading at Mass is usually taken from the Old Testament.

During the Easter season, the first reading is taken from the New Testament, from the Acts of the Apostles. This book tells the story of the church when it was very new, just after the resurrection of Jesus and the coming of the Holy Spirit at Pentecost.

No matter what book the first reading comes from, the first reading is chosen to relate to the Gospel reading in some way. The two stories go together, and help us understand something important about God and ourselves.

Something to Know

- **The Bible** — Our sacred Scriptures. A collection of seventy-two books that contains inspired stories of how God saves us.

- **The Old Testament** — contains forty-five of these books, telling the story of God's salvation *before* Jesus.

- **The Lectionary** — the large book the lector reads from at Mass. It is not the whole Bible, but it contains the parts of the Bible (the Scripture readings) that are proclaimed in the liturgy.

- **The Lector** — the person who proclaims the first and second Scripture readings at Mass. The lector might also announce the intercessions during the Prayer of the Faithful.

- **The Ambo** — The place in church where the Scripture is proclaimed. It may also be called the *pulpit* or the *lectern*.

- **The Response** — At the end of the first and second reading, the lector says: "The Word of the Lord." We respond: "Thanks be to God." (See the *Roman Missal* or sacramentary).

Living Our Liturgy

The word of God has the power to make us different—if we listen. Through the Scriptures, God speaks to us. God shapes us so that we know God's way and follow it better.

But sometimes the Scripture readings are hard to understand, even for adults. We can listen better if we are prepared in advance. The best way to do this is to read the Sunday Scriptures at home during the week.

Something to Do

With your group, read the first reading for the *coming* Sunday. Use this space to tell about the reading.

What book is the reading taken from? _____

What chapter _____

What verses? _____

How do you feel when you hear this reading? Why? _____

_____

_____

_____

What message do you find in this reading? _____

_____

_____

What is your favorite line in the reading? Why did you pick that one?

_____

_____

_____

After Mass this weekend, tell how the first reading is related to the Gospel:

_____

_____

_____

Listen to the homily carefully when you are at Mass this coming weekend. Perhaps you will hear the preacher speak about some of the ideas *you* had when you read this passage!

In Our Parish

- When you go to Mass, be able to point out the ambo.

- Is the ambo similar in style to the altar? Why might the ambo and the altar look similar?

- Do you know anyone who is a lector? Ask him or her how they prepare to proclaim the Scriptures. If you don't know any lectors, you and your folks could introduce yourselves to the lector at Mass this weekend. Ask the lector to show you the lectionary and talk with him or her bout this ministry.

_____

_____

_____

Notes

This handout taken from
Learning about Liturgy,
© 2001 Dorothy Kosinski Carola.
All rights reserved.

LEARNING ABOUT
Liturgy

Liturgy of the Word: Psalm

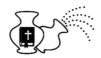

Our Lives

Andrew had never seen such a fancy invitation. It was printed with curly writing and decorated with pretty flowers. And there were so many pieces! Inside the envelope was a second envelope; inside that was the invitation. Inside *that* was a smaller envelope and a smaller card.

"What's all this for?" Andrew asked his dad. "This is the invitation to Aunt Kathy's wedding. We'll send in our response on this smaller card." Andrew was confused. "But Aunt Kathy already knows we're coming. I'm a junior usher and you're going to be one of the lectors." "You're right, sort of," Dad answered. "We've responded to Aunt Kathy before, but this is the formal invitation and we have to send in our formal response."

Our Liturgy

In our relationship with God, we constantly make our response to God by the way we live. In liturgy, as with the wedding invitation, we respond in a ritual way. After the first reading, the cantor leads us in singing one of the psalms. It might be a different psalm each week, or we could sing the same psalm for several weeks. Usually, the psalm is sung in "call-and-response" form. That means that the cantor and the assembly take turns singing back and forth. That's why it is called the *responsorial psalm*. The psalm is a good example of how God is active in the Liturgy of the Word: God's word calls us and we answer.

The psalm is also our response to the word of God we have just heard in the first reading. The psalm is chosen to go with the first

"Let the peoples praise you, O God; let all the peoples praise you."

—Ps 67:3

This handout taken from
Learning about Liturgy,
© 2001 Dorothy Kosinski Carola.
All rights reserved.

reading, which is related to the Gospel. So when we sing the psalm, we are taking the word of God for that day into our hearts.

The psalms are found in the Old Testament. They are prayers that were used in ancient Jewish worship. There are sad psalms and happy psalms. Some psalms praise God's goodness, while others cry out to God for help. There are psalms that ask forgiveness and psalms that ask for healing. You will find psalms that give thanks for God's help, and psalms that beg God to fix all the evil in the world. You can find a psalm for just about every occasion or mood.

When the Jewish people prayed the psalms at worship, they sang them, and so do we. Singing is a wonderful way to pray because when we sing our prayer, we use more of our mind and more of our heart to praise God. St. Augustine once said, "Those who sing, pray twice."

You will notice that the cantor leads the psalm from the same place as the lector and the priest read the Scriptures. That's because the psalm is Scripture too. We use that one special place in church for the Liturgy of the Word and *only* for the Liturgy of the Word.

Something to Know

- The Bible contains **150 psalms**.

- The **cantor** is the person who leads us in singing the psalm at Mass. This person might also be called the **psalmist.**

Living Our Liturgy

You can use the psalms when you pray by yourself too. You can pray this psalm to thank God for the gift of Sunday worship.

Psalm 84:2,3,4–5,10

Deep in my heart I long
for your temple,
and with all that I am
I sing joyful songs to you.

LORD God All-Powerful,
my King and my God,
sparrows find a home
near your altars;
swallows build nests there
to raise their young.

You bless everyone
who lives in your house,
and they sing your praises.
You bless all who depend
on you for their strength
and all who deeply desire
to visit your temple.

One day in your temple
is better than a thousand
anywhere else.
I would rather serve
in your house,
than live in the homes
of the wicked.

From the Contemporary English Version © American Bible Society. Used by permission. As found in the *Lectionary for Masses with Children.*

Here is a psalm you can pray when you feel troubled.

Psalm 130:1–2,3–4,5,6d–7a

From a sea of troubles
I call out to you, LORD.
Won't you please listen
as I beg for mercy?

If you kept record of our sins,
no one could last long.
But you forgive us,
and so we will worship you.

With all my heart,
I am waiting, LORD, for you!
I trust your promises.
Yes, I wait more eagerly
than a soldier on guard duty
waits for the dawn.
Israel, trust in the LORD!

From the Contemporary English Version © American Bible Society. Used by permission. As found in the *Lectionary for Masses with Children.*

Here is a joyful psalm you can pray to show your trust in God:

Psalm 27:1,4,13–14

> You, LORD, are the light
> that keeps me safe.
> I am not afraid of anyone.
> You protect me,
> and I have no fears.
>
> I ask only one thing, LORD:
> Let me live in your house
> every day of my life
> to see how wonderful you are
> and to pray in your temple.
>
> I know that I will live
> to see how kind you are.
> Trust the Lord!
> Be brave and strong
> and trust the Lord.

From the Contemporary English Version © American Bible Society. Used by permission. As found in the *Lectionary for Masses with Children*.

Pray these psalms with your family, or before you go to bed. You may find other psalms in the Bible that you would like to add to your prayers.

 In Our Parish

- Is the psalm sung at Sunday liturgies?
- Who is (are) the cantor(s)?
- Does your parish sing a different psalm every week, or do you sing the same psalm or a period of weeks or a season?

_____

Notes

LEARNING ABOUT
Liturgy

Liturgy of the Word: Second Reading

"Indeed, the Word of God is living and active."

—Heb 4:12

Our Lives

"It's Mom, calling from San Jose," Matt called to his sister. Megan picked up the extension in the other room. "How's your business trip going?" she asked. "Just fine," Mom replied, "But I really want to know how all of you are doing. Are you being helpful to Grandma?" "We are," they answered together. "How about your homework? Matt, did you finish reading that novel you were working on for class?" "Well, I did some reading the other day. I think I'm up to page 107," Matt explained. Mom was concerned. "You need to be writing your report on that book this weekend. You should be reading an hour a day if you're going to get it done on time. I'm hoping you'll finish it before I get home on Saturday afternoon. That way, we'll have Sunday to catch up with each other, and no homework to fuss with." Matt understood. "That's the only homework I have, so I'll spend lots of time on it before you get home."

Megan chimed in: "I'm kind of worried about tomorrow's math test. I wish you were here to help me study." "I know Grandma can help you with that," Mom assured her. "And we did plenty of work on the multiplication tables right before I left. Just study and I'm sure you'll do fine."

Megan and Matt were glad to have spoken with their Mom. Matt knew he had to work hard on his book report. Megan felt more confident about her math test.

Our Liturgy

It is important for people to keep in touch with each other, even when they are far away. Today we can do this with phone calls or e-mail, but when the Church was young, the only way to keep in touch was by writing letters. Saint Paul and the other disciples stayed in touch with other Christian communities and other Christian leaders. As St. Paul traveled to many lands preaching the Good News of Jesus Christ, he wrote letters to the Christian communities he had already visited. He wrote to help them understand their Christian faith and to help them live better Christian lives. These letters are in the Bible. The second reading at Mass, after the psalm, is often a piece of one of those letters.

Just as Matt and Megan's mom offered advise and encouragement, St. Paul did the same with the newly formed Christian communities. Sometimes, disagreements would arise in a community, and St. Paul would write with advice about solving the disagreement. Sometimes, the early Christians found it difficult to keep their new faith. St. Paul wrote to encourage them and remind them of what Jesus' death and resurrection means. Sometimes the letters were written to a particular person rather than a whole community. No matter who the recipient was, the letters in the Bible all have a similar purpose.

Most of the time, the second reading is not related to the first reading and the Gospel reading. It has an important message for us, but not the same message as the other readings. During Ordinary Time, the second reading is a more or less continuous reading from one or more of Paul's letters. During the special seasons of Advent, Christmas, Lent, and Easter, the second reading more closely corresponds to the other two.

Something to Know

- The letters written by St. Paul are: the Letter to the Romans, the First Letter to the Corinthians, the Second Letter to the Corinthians, the Letter to the Galatians, the Letter to the Ephesians, the Letter to the Philippians, the Letter to the Colossians, the First Letter to the Thessalonians, the Second Letter to the Thessalonians, the First Letter to Timothy, the Second Letter to Timothy, the Letter to Titus, and the Letter to Philemon.

- Letters written by other early disciples are the Letter to the Hebrews, the Letter of James, the First Letter of Peter, the Second Letter of Peter, the First Letter of John, the Second Letter of John, the Third Letter of John, and the Letter of Jude.

- Sometimes the second reading is taken from a book that is not a letter. The Acts of the Apostles tells the story of the early church. The Book of Revelation, the last book of the Bible, is a symbolic book about the final days.

Living Our Liturgy

We know that the Bible is the inspired word of God. So when we hear a reading from one of St. Paul's letters, for example, it's as though God were sending us a letter to help us on our journey.

The Scriptures are our best guide for right living. Listen carefully when the Scriptures are proclaimed at Mass. Slowly but surely you will come to know God's ways and live them just as Jesus did.

Something to Do

With your group, read the New Testament reading for the *coming* Sunday. Use this space to tell about the reading.

What book is the reading taken from? _____

What chapter? _____

What verses? _____

How do you feel when you hear this reading? Why? _____

_____

_____

What message do you find in this reading? _____

_____

_____

What is your favorite line in the reading? Why did you pick that one?

_____

_____

_____

Listen to the homily carefully when you are at Mass this coming weekend. Perhaps you will hear the preacher speak about some of the ideas *you* had when you read these passages!

This handout taken from *Learning about Liturgy,* © 2001 Dorothy Kosinski Carola. All rights reserved.

In Our Parish

Does one lector proclaim the first reading and another the second? Or does one lector proclaim both readings? Can you find out why your parish does it this way?

_____

_____

_____

_____

Notes

LEARNING ABOUT
Liturgy

Liturgy of the Word: Gospel

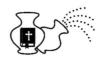

Our Lives

Samantha wanted to be the first one to tell her dad the good news. It was important news, so she did not go off to play with her friends. She just stood by the door waiting for her dad to get home from work. As she saw him walking up the street from the bus stop, Samantha ran to meet him. "I have good news!" Samantha exclaimed. "Grandpa's operation went really well and he's going to be just fine! Aunt Michele says he'll be home next week!"

Our Liturgy

There is good news to tell at Mass, too. It is the Good News of Jesus.

When it is time to hear the Good News, we stand up. This is the most important Scripture reading at Mass. Because it is so special, we sing an acclamation before the Gospel (usually an "Alleluia"). We have a procession with the Book of the Gospels. This is our way of showing our reverence for this most important part of God's word. Our singing shows the joyful anticipation we feel when we are about to hear the Gospel.

Week by week, the story of Jesus' life, death, and resurrection unfolds. We hear the story of Jesus' work on earth. We hear of his teachings and his miracles. We hear of his relationship with God the Father and of his relationship with his disciples. We hear how people reacted to Jesus: Some believed he was the Messiah; others had him killed.

Most important, in the Gospels we hear that Jesus has power over evil. The way of Jesus is stronger than the way of sin. Evil has no permanent power.

Jesus was completely faithful to God's way. He preached the truth of God even when it meant he would be crucified for it. But God was faithful to Jesus. God raised Jesus from the dead. Because of this, we can be sure that God's way is more powerful than the evil we see around us. When we live God's law of love, we can be certain it is the best way. We are God's children through baptism, and God has promised to do for us what he did for Jesus. We too have eternal life. We too will be raised up on the last day when Christ comes again.

 ## Something to Know

- **Gospel** — means "good news"

- **The Book of the Gospels** — the large book that the priest or deacon reads from at Mass. It contains the parts of the Gospels (the Gospel readings) that are proclaimed at liturgy.

- **The Four Gospels** — the Gospel of Matthew, the Gospel of Mark, the Gospel of Luke, and the Gospel of John. The Gospels were written thirty to seventy years after Jesus' resurrection. They were written by close followers of Jesus, or by the followers who came after them.

- **Cycles A, B, and C** — At Mass we hear the Gospels in a three-year cycle. That means that the Scripture readings you hear at Mass this week will not be read again for another three years. In Year A we hear the Gospel of Matthew. In Year B we hear the Gospel of Mark. In Year C we hear the Gospel of Luke. The Gospel of John is read at different times during each of these years, mostly during the Easter season.

- **The proclamation of the Gospel** — The cantor sings an "Alleluia" with an antiphon in call-and-response style. Everyone stands. The assembly responds by singing the second and third alleluias. (During Lent, we do not use alleluia. We use "Praise to you, Lord Jesus Christ, king of endless glory" or another acclamation.)

  While the acclamation is sung, the priest or deacon carries the Book of the Gospels to the ambo.

The priest or deacon says:	The Lord be with you.
We say:	*And also with you.*
The priest or deacon says:	A reading from the holy Gospel according to *(name of Gospel).*
We say:	*Glory to you, Lord.*

After the proclamation of the Gospel:

The priest or deacon says: The Gospel of the Lord.

We say: *Praise to you, Lord Jesus Christ.*

Living Our Liturgy

Samantha was eager to tell her dad the good news about her grandfather. Are we as eager as Samantha to share *our* Good News about Jesus? There are many people who need to hear it. People who are treated badly need to hear that Jesus accepts everyone. People who have done wrong need to hear that Jesus is forgiving. People who are unhappy need to hear about Jesus' way to happiness. People who feel alone need to know that Jesus is their friend.

Something to Do

With your group, read the Gospel passage for the *coming* Sunday.

What book is the reading taken from? _____

What chapter? _____

What verses? _____

How do you feel when you hear this reading? Why? _____

_____

_____

_____

_____

What message do you find in this reading? _____

_____

_____

_____

When we hear good news, we want to tell others about it. What are some ways you let others know about the Good News of Jesus?

_____

_____

_____

_____

Listen to the homily carefully when you are at Mass this coming weekend. Perhaps you will hear the preacher speak about some of the ideas *you* had when you read this passage!

In Our Parish

- What lectionary cycle is it this year?

_____

- What Gospel is being read at Mass during this cycle?

_____

- Do one or more deacons sometimes proclaim the Gospel at Mass? What are their names?

_____

_____

_____

Notes

LEARNING ABOUT
Liturgy

Liturgy of the Word: Homily, Creed, and Prayer of the Faithful

Our Lives

The Scout Troop was ready for the big camping trip. For three days, they would be hiking a portion of the Appalachian Trail and making camp in the wilderness. Some of the younger Scouts were nervous. They had never hiked such a long way. They had very little experience in wilderness living.

The older Scouts reassured them; they had made this trip before. Just a few days earlier, two Scouts had checked out the conditions on the trail. They knew where they were going. They knew the best places to make camp. They knew many of the dangers and how to avoid them. They could help the younger Scouts who had trouble with steep climbs or with pitching their tents. With the more experienced Scouts as guides, everyone would be able to enjoy the journey.

At the end of the first day's hike, the troop made camp. Sitting around the fire that night, they recited the Scout Oath together. Then they spoke about the day's experience. Many of the younger Scouts were amazed that they had made it. They had done something they didn't know they could do. They had seen things they had never seen before. They had worked together and grown closer as a troop. They felt more confident as they looked forward to the adventures of the next two days.

"They devoted themselves to the apostles' teaching and fellowship, to the breaking of the bread and the prayers."

—Acts 2:42

Our Liturgy

When all of the Scriptures have been proclaimed, the priest or deacon gives a **homily**. The person who preaches is like a guide on an adventurous journey. Through the homily, the homilist guides us on our journey with God. Just like the older Scouts preparing for the hike, the homilist is well prepared to guide us. He studies and prays with the Scripture all the time. He can show us the wonderful things God is trying to communicate to us through the Scriptures of the day. He explains the Scriptures in the homily and helps us realize how they apply to our lives. He helps us understand what these Scriptures tell us about God and about how to live God's way.

Following the homily, there is a period of silence. Like the quiet time after the readings, this helps us reflect on everything we have just heard in the Liturgy of the Word.

Next comes the Creed. The Creed is our summary of all that we believe. Usually, we say the Nicene Creed, but we could say the Apostles' Creed instead.

The final element of the Liturgy of the Word is the prayer of the faithful. Another name for the prayer of the faithful is the universal prayer, or the general intercessions. These are prayers of petition, which means they are *asking* prayers. We ask for God's help on our journey. We ask God to help those who are in need. We bring the needs of all the world to God in these prayers.

The prayer intentions are announced by a deacon, lector, or priest. Usually, each prayer consists of a short petition that states a need, and then a short response for the assembly. For example:

That the church will spread the Good News of Jesus to people of every nation, we pray.
Lord, hear our prayer.

For an end to hatred between peoples and nations, we pray.
Grant it, O Lord, we humbly pray.

That all those who are hungry will find the help they need in God's people, we pray.
Hear us, O Lord.

For this holy assembly, may we experience God's love in this Eucharist, we pray.
Gracious God, grant our prayer.

You will notice a pattern in the way we offer our petitions. We pray for:

- The church

- The world

- People in need

- The local community

Of course, that doesn't mean there will only be four petitions. There may be more than one in any category. It is also customary to include a petition for those who are sick and for those who have died.

Some of the petitions might be related to the Scriptures. For instance, when we hear the Gospel about the Good Samaritan, we might pray that we stop judging people who are different from us. When we pray for people in need, we might include some local needs and some worldwide needs. Perhaps a fire in your town left several people homeless. Maybe a recent hurricane caused great damage in a foreign country. All these needs can be mentioned in the Prayer of the Faithful.

Now, the Liturgy of the Word is concluded. Like the Scouts at the end of their first day, we are stronger Christians, we are a closer community, and we are prepared for what is to come. We are ready to enter into the Liturgy of the Eucharist.

Something to Know

- **Homily** — the talk about the Scriptures (or sometimes, about one of the prayers of the Mass) that the priest or deacon gives after the Gospel.

- **Homilist** — the person who gives the homily. This person can also be called the "preacher."

- **Preaching** — what a priest or deacon is doing when he's giving a homily.

- **Petition** — an urgent request. In the prayer of the faithful, each of the short prayers is called a petition.

- **Intercession** — a request that you make not for yourself, but for someone else. The petitions of the prayer of the faithful are also called intercessions, because we are asking God to help other people. We *intercede* for them.

Living Our Liturgy

We are all like Scouts on the same journey. Each time we are nourished with the word of God at the liturgy, we take a few more steps on our journey with God. Working together, and with good guides, each person comes to know God better.

Something to Do

With your group, read the Scriptures for the *coming* week. Then write some petitions that fit with those readings. Don't forget to consider world and local needs. What is going on in your own community that needs prayer?

In Our Parish

- Is there a children's Liturgy of the Word? If so, what ages are the children who attend? How does this help the children?

- Which Creed is used, the Nicene Creed or the Apostles' Creed? Can you say it by heart?

- Who prepares the prayer of the faithful for the weekend liturgies?

- What is the response to the prayer of the faithful? Does it change every week, or is it the same for several weeks in a row?

Notes

This handout taken from
Learning about Liturgy,
© 2001 Dorothy Kosinski Carola.
All rights reserved.

LEARNING ABOUT
Liturgy

Lesson 10 Handout

Liturgy of the Eucharist: Overview of Meal and Sacrifice

Our Lives

Everyone applauded as Grandma and Grandpa walked back down the center aisle. Elizabeth followed with her cousin Michael, then came Aunt Judy and Uncle Gus. The rest of the family and friends lined up to congratulate Grandma and Grandpa on celebrating their fiftieth wedding anniversary. When everyone had left the church, they set off for the restaurant where they would dance and eat and celebrate.

While they were having dinner, Elizabeth leaned over to her grandmother. She commented: "It was really nice to hear you renew your wedding vows, even though you weren't really getting married." Grandma thought for a minute. "Well, it felt pretty real to me. In fact, those vows meant more today than they did fifty years ago. Today seems like my wedding day all over again. I'm really glad you could be here this time."

Our Liturgy

Our liturgy is often referred to as a "sacrificial meal." This simple phrase gives us two important ways to think about the Liturgy of the Eucharist. Like the anniversary dinner, people with something special to celebrate gather for a meal. And like the

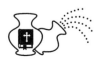

"While they were eating, Jesus took a loaf of bread, and after blessing it he broke it, gave it to the disciples, and said, 'Take, eat; this is my body.' Then he took a cup, and after giving thanks he gave it to them, saying, 'Drink from it, all of you; for this is my blood of the covenant, which is poured out for many for the forgiveness of sins.'"

—Mt 26:26–28

renewal of vows, it feels pretty real—just like the sacrifice Jesus made for us on the cross.

The Mass Is a Meal

Sharing a meal has always been an important way for people to celebrate and become united with one another. We can hardly imagine a special celebration that does not include food! Eating together draws people closer. Whether it's sharing a candy bar or a Thanksgiving feast, we are joined to those with whom we eat.

During his life, Jesus shared many meals with his friends. When he was accused of eating with sinners, Jesus preached about God's welcoming compassion for sinners. When he appeared to his disciples after his resurrection, he made breakfast for them. When his followers were hungry, he blessed five loaves of bread and two fish and fed more than five thousand people. When he went to a great banquet, he preached about sitting in the lowest place. There are many examples of meals Jesus shared with others in the Gospels.

It is not surprising, then, that Jesus chose a meal as the way in which he wants to be remembered. Just as he did at the Last Supper, Jesus calls his followers to the table every Sunday to share a meal with him.

The elements of a meal are easy to see in the liturgy. We can see that the altar is a table. We can see that the bread and wine are food and drink. They are consecrated and given back to us as the food and drink of eternal life. Eating and drinking are two of the central actions of the liturgy. That's why the church offers communion in both forms. By eating and drinking, we are remembering Jesus in the way in which he asked to be remembered.

Something to Do

Compare our celebration of Eucharist to a special meal. In the right-hand column, tell how what happens at liturgy is like what happens at a special meal.

At a special meal:	At a Mass:
We invite people to join us.	_____
We greet our guests.	_____
We share our stories.	_____
We set the table.	_____
We get the food ready.	_____
We eat and drink.	_____
We clear the table.	_____

The Mass Is a Sacrifice

Just as there are many examples of meals Jesus shared in the Gospels, there are also many examples of the sacrifices Jesus made for people. He left his home in order to preach to the people. People criticized him for welcoming sinners and showing them God's compassion, but he made that sacrifice so that even the outcasts would know God's love. By curing people on the sabbath, he broke the sabbath laws and gave up being accepted by the Jewish leaders. The supreme sacrifice, of course, was when he gave up his life instead of giving up God's way.

Sacrifices have an important place in Jewish history. In Old Testament days, kings would sacrifice an animal when they made a covenant, or agreement, with each other. Farmers would sacrifice their first produce or their best lamb as a sign of their gratitude and trust in God.

The Passover sacrifice of a lamb was the most important sacrifice of the Jewish year. When the Israelites were slaves in Egypt, God sent an angel to kill every firstborn son in Egypt. The blood of a lamb smeared on their doors saved the Israelites from this plague. When the Pharaoh saw what had happened, the Israelites were set free.

Because Jesus' crucifixion happened at Passover, Jesus' sacrifice of himself reminded the early Christians of the Passover lamb. As the blood of the lamb saved the Israelites, the blood of Jesus saves us. As the lamb was the sacrifice of the first covenant, Jesus is the sacrifice of the New Covenant. When we were slaves to sin, the blood Jesus shed on the cross saved us. We are set free from sin by the covenant God makes with us in Jesus. So at Mass, when the consecrated bread is broken and the consecrated wine is poured out, we sing about Jesus as the "Lamb of God" who takes away the sins of the world.

Just as Elizabeth's grandmother felt as if it were her wedding day, the sacrifice of Jesus is present again in every liturgy. Through the power of the Holy Spirit, the bread that is broken and the wine that is poured out become the Body of Jesus that is broken and the Blood of Jesus that is poured out for us. What happened on Calvary is happening again, only now it is an un-bloody sacrifice. And this time, we can be there.

Living Our Liturgy

We are asked to make many sacrifices in our lives. Like Jesus, we might have to give up being accepted in order to do what is right. Like Jesus, we might be criticized for treating someone nicely even though no one else does. Missionaries still leave their homes to preach the Good News to those who have not yet heard it. And though it is not too common, people still give their lives for living God's way. Can you think of some examples?

Something to Do

Every sacrifice we make unites us with Jesus. In this space, give some examples of sacrifices you have to make. How do these sacrifices show love?

_____

_____

_____

_____

_____

_____

In Our Parish

- Can you clearly see the consecrated bread being broken and the consecrated wine being poured?

- Can you sing the "Lamb of God" litany your parish uses during the breaking and the pouring?

_____

Notes

LEARNING ABOUT
Liturgy

Lesson 11 Handout

Liturgy of the Eucharist: Giving Thanks

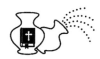

Our Lives

"Manny, would you please stay behind after dismissal?" Mr. Rosario asked. Manuel's heart sank deeper. He was already confused about the homework assignment. Now he thought he was in trouble too.

Mr. Rosario began. "Manuel, I thought I saw a funny look on your face when I was describing the reading assignment. Do you need to ask a question about it?" Manuel was surprised that his teacher had noticed. "Mr. Rosario, I really didn't get what you were talking about, but I was so confused I couldn't even think of a question," Manuel explained. "Why don't you get out your book and your notes from today's class and I'll show you what I mean," Mr. Rosario offered. "Well, if you have time," Manuel answered shyly. "I just want you to do well, so don't worry about my time." Mr. Rosario smiled.

Manuel was surprised at his teacher's generosity. He had always liked Mr. Rosario, but suddenly Manuel realized just how hard he worked for his students. When Manuel went home, he finally understood the assignment. More important, he was really grateful to Mr. Rosario for looking out for him.

One of the first things parents teach their children is how to say "thank you." Sometimes we say "thank you," just to be polite. It is good to say "thank you," even when someone gives you a present you don't like or one you already have. But it is more important to notice the wonderful things people do for us. We need to notice when people are kind and helpful. Then gratitude will be more than just *saying* "thank you." Being grateful will be a way of life for us.

"Thanks be to God, who gives us the victory through our Lord Jesus Christ."

—1 Cor 15:57

Our Liturgy

Throughout salvation history, God's people have been surprised over and over and over again at the wonderful ways in which God is looking out for us. The gratitude we feel is expressed in the Liturgy of the Eucharist.

There are many ways in which the Liturgy of the Eucharist expresses thanks. In the collection, we give some portion of the gifts we have received. The sacrifice we make in the collection is part of our prayer of gratitude to God. It is also an important way for us to take part in the work of the church.

A few people from the assembly bring the gifts of bread and wine, along with the people's sacrificial offering, to the altar. There, the priest presents them to God with a prayer of thanksgiving, which he may say quietly or out loud:

Blessed are you, Lord God of all creation.
Through your goodness we have this bread to offer,
which earth has given and human hands have made.
It will become for us the bread of life.

Blessed are you, Lord God of all creation.
Through your goodness we have this wine to offer,
fruit of the vine and work of human hands.
It will become our spiritual drink.

Each time, we respond: *"Blessed be God forever."*

With this prayer at the preparation of the gifts (see the sacramentary), we praise God for his goodness to us. We give thanks for the gifts of creation, and for our own creation. We are grateful that God's gifts of wheat and grapes, plus our own work, have made bread and wine to offer to God for this Eucharist.

Our thanksgiving continues as the eucharistic prayer begins. The preface prayer thanks God for his gift of Jesus. There are many prefaces, but here is one example (Sundays in Ordinary Time I, from the sacramentary):

Father, all-powerful and ever-living God,
we do well always and everywhere to give you thanks
through Jesus Christ our Lord.

Through his cross and resurrection
he freed us from sin and death
and called us to the glory that has made us
 a chosen race, a royal priesthood, a people set apart.

Everywhere we proclaim your mighty works
for you have called us out of darkness
into your own wonderful light.

And so, with all the choirs of angels in heaven
we proclaim your glory
and join in their unending hymn of praise:

Then we sing "Holy, Holy, Holy," an acclamation of praise to God.

Something to Know

- The word **"Eucharist"** comes from a Greek word that means "thanksgiving."

- **Sacramentary** — A large red book containing the priest's prayers for the liturgy. There is an opening prayer and a prayer after communion for every day, many prefaces and several eucharistic prayers, blessings, and Masses for special occasions. You will usually see the sacramentary on the altar during the Liturgy of the Eucharist.

- **The parts of the Liturgy of the Eucharist are:**
Preparation of the Altar
Presentation of the Gifts
Preface
Holy, Holy, Holy
Eucharistic Prayer
    Memorial Acclamation
    Consecration
    Doxology
    Great Amen
Our Father
Sign of Peace
Lamb of God
Communion
Prayer after Communion

Living Our Liturgy

When we make thanksgiving a way of life, we will pray the Eucharist with more meaning. We need to practice becoming grateful people.

Something to Do

Each day be on the lookout for something to be grateful for. You will probably find many things every day. Use this space for a "Gratitude Inventory." Write down what you are grateful for each day:

Sunday: _____

_____

This handout taken from
Learning about Liturgy,
© 2001 Dorothy Kosinski Carola.
All rights reserved.

Monday: _____

_____

Tuesday: _____

_____

Wednesday: _____

_____

Thursday: _____

_____

Friday: _____

_____

Saturday: _____

   Don't forget to praise and thank God each day for all the people and things in your "inventory."

In Our Parish

   After Mass, ask the priest to show you the sacramentary and where the different prayers of the Mass are found in it.

_____

Notes

This handout taken from
Learning about Liturgy,
© 2001 Dorothy Kosinski Carola.
All rights reserved.

Lesson 12 Handout

Liturgy of the Eucharist: Remembering and Ritual

"For as often as you eat this bread and drink the cup, you proclaim the Lord's death until he comes."

—1 Cor 11:26

Our Lives: Seeing What's on the Inside

If you know someone really well, you can probably tell how he or she feels just by looking at him or her. You might be able to look at your friend's face and see that she is upset. You can probably take one look at your teacher and tell if he is angry.

Human beings *need* to express on the outside what they are feeling and believing on the inside. That's why we can tell how a person feels even without words: what we think and feel shows in how we walk and in our faces. Others can often tell just by looking.

Ritual

Today was Allison's twelfth birthday, but it didn't feel like much of a birthday to her. It was a Thursday, so she had to go to school. Nothing special about that! She used to bring cupcakes for her class, but this year she told her mom she was "too old" for that. Only her two closest friends remembered that it was her birthday. Right after school, Allison went to her religious education class. When she finally got home, she had extra math homework and a science test to study for. Her mom made a special dessert, but they were not having a cake with candles until Saturday. That's when her grandparents, aunts and uncles and cousins would be coming for the *real* party.

When Saturday came, the house was decorated with balloons and birthday banners. Her younger brother had even made a special birthday card for her on the computer at school. Her mom was preparing her favorite foods, and family members arrived with gifts. Her grandmother passed around a photo album that showed pictures of Allison since she was born. Everyone remarked about how much she had grown and changed.

Finally, Allison saw the beautiful cake with twelve candles lit. Everyone sang "Happy Birthday." She made a wish and blew out the candles. Allison had always made the first cut in the cake, but this year she was old enough to do all the cutting herself. Everyone was happy they were together to celebrate Allison's birth. Allison was happy to be who she was, and her family was happy she belonged to them.

After her guests had left, Allison remarked to her mom: "I know my birthday was Thursday, but today really *felt* like my birthday!"

Our Liturgy

For many centuries, the church has been reflecting on the life, death, and resurrection of Jesus. The Holy Spirit is constantly at work in our lives to help us pray and reflect about what this means. The second half of Mass *shows* us what the church believes. When we are at Mass, it is like looking at the church's face to see what we believe and feel on the inside. When we do liturgy really well, we *should* be able to tell what the church believes just by looking.

Just as with Allison's birthday, the real meaning of Jesus for us is expressed when we do the ritual. Allison knew it was her birthday on Thursday, but it didn't *feel* that way. The birthday rituals helped her *experience* what her birthday really meant. And she needed to be with the people who were really glad she was born.

In the same way, we know that Jesus died, was raised, and remains with us now. The ritual that is the Mass lets us *experience* what this really means in our lives. We need to be with the people who love Jesus as we do. When we pray the prayers and sing the songs and do the gestures that make up our ritual, Jesus is present with us. Allison's birthday became *real* because of the birthday rituals. Our life with Jesus becomes *real* because of the Mass. Every time we do the ritual, we are proclaiming Jesus' reign. We are proclaiming our faith that Jesus has conquered sin and death, and will come again in glory.

Something to Know

- **Gesture** — movement that has meaning

- **Ritual** — actions that have meaning; a series of formal or prescribed actions that express our beliefs.

Living Our Liturgy

This is how the liturgy shapes and forms us. Every week, we have the chance to be with Jesus and his people. Over and over, the liturgy allows us to experience God's action in our lives and the meaning of Jesus for us. The liturgy can grow and change, and we can grow and change, so we will find new meanings and new insights throughout our lives.

Something to Do

1. Think of a ritual that has nothing to do with church or religion. Why do people do this ritual? What is this ritual supposed to express?

_____

_____

_____

_____

_____

2. Suppose Allison's mother had decided that it would be good to do something different for Allison's birthday for a change. So there would be no cake, no candles, and no "Happy Birthday" song this year. Instead, all the guests would sit backward on their chairs. They would eat only salad and use only spoons. Do you think this new ritual would help Allison *feel* as if it was her birthday? Explain:

_____

_____

_____

_____

This handout taken from
Learning about Liturgy,
© 2001 Dorothy Kosinski Carola.
All rights reserved.

In Our Parish

- Have you noticed any changes in the way liturgy is done at your parish recently? Are these permanent changes or seasonal changes? Can you find out why the changes were made?

- What postures does the assembly use during the eucharistic prayer? Can you tell what these postures mean? Outline when your assembly changes position:

Stand _____

_____

Kneel _____

_____

Sit _____

_____

Notes

LEARNING ABOUT
Liturgy

Liturgy of the Eucharist: Remembering and Making Present

"Do this in remembrance of me."

—Lk 22:19

Our Lives

Your memory is a very helpful gift. You can remember how to get around your neighborhood without getting lost. You can remember how to spell the words for your spelling test. You *may* even remember where you put your shoes when you last took them off!

Recalling information is only one way we use our memory. There is another way in which memory works, though. Memory can help us relive and re-feel events that have happened in the past. Memory can make those events happen again.

What are some of your favorite memories? Close your eyes and picture your favorite place, or last year's summer vacation, or a good time you had with friends. How does it feel? How does it look? Doesn't it seem as though you really *are* there, as though the event really *is* happening again? That's because it is—through the power of memory.

Ritual and Memory

We may use more than just our imaginations to remember. Often we use ritual as well. Remember the story of Allison's birthday? The birthday rituals helped her and her family make the memory of her birth and childhood come alive again.

Here is another example of how memory and ritual work together to bring out the true meaning of an event:

The Ruiz family had just come home from Christmas Eve Mass. This was always an exciting moment. The youngest child was now allowed to place the statue of the infant Jesus in the crib of the nativity scene. Mariela was only four, but she held the figurine very carefully. She already knew how special this nativity set was. It used to belong to her grandmother in Mexico. Mrs. Ruiz was very honored that her mother had let her bring it with her when she came to the United States.

The family sang while Mariela walked slowly through the living room, knelt by the crib, and placed the infant Jesus on the straw. Then, just as she did every year, Mrs. Ruiz talked about her own Christmas memories, about coming to this country, and about how much she misses her mother. The Ruiz children have never met their grandmother, but they feel close to her when they set up her *nacimiento*. They grow in their love for each other. The remembering and the ritual bring the real meaning of family to life for them.

Our Liturgy

The remembering we do during the eucharistic prayer is like the remembering in the Ruiz family when they prepare their nativity scene. The church's memory and the church's ritual bring the real meaning of our faith to life again. We don't just *recall* that Jesus died and was raised from the dead. It is not just a past event, something that is over. Through the power of the Holy Spirit, our remembering and our ritual bring that reality into the present. It is happening again. The covenant Jesus made with us is being made again. We become part of the life of Jesus through the liturgy. We put on Jesus' life as though it were our own. We call this *entering into the paschal mystery*. Just as with the Ruiz family, we don't just remember. We become part of what we remember.

That's why we hear lots about remembering in the eucharistic prayer. We always tell the story of Jesus' Last Supper. Then we sing a memorial acclamation that sums up what we believe:

A. Christ has died, Christ is risen, Christ will come again.

B. Dying, you destroyed our death rising you restored our life. Lord Jesus come in glory.

C. When we eat this bread and drink this cup, we proclaim your death, Lord Jesus, until you come in glory.

D. Lord, by your cross and resurrection you have set us free. You are the Savior of the world.

Then we continue to remember, like this:

In memory of his death and resurrection,
we offer you, Father, this life-giving bread,
this saving cup (*Eucharistic Prayer II*).

Father, calling to mind the death your Son endured for
    our salvation,
his glorious resurrection and ascension into heaven,
and ready to greet him when he comes again,
we offer you in thanksgiving this holy and living sacrifice
(*Eucharistic Prayer III*).

We do now what Jesus told us to do.
We remember his death and his resurrection
and we offer you, Father, the bread that gives us life,
and the cup that saves us
(*Eucharistic Prayer I for Masses with Children*).

Something to Know

• **Paschal mystery** — the life, death and resurrection of Jesus, by which we are saved.

• **Paschal** — means *Easter.* It comes from the Hebrew word *pesach,* which means *Passover.*

• **Mystery** — God's plan for our salvation, which we can't figure out by ourselves. It can only be revealed to us by God.

Living Our Liturgy

Through the liturgy, we are more and more able to put on Jesus' life as though it were our own. But this is a very big job. Jesus' life was one of compassion and faithfulness. He did not abandon God's ways, even when he was criticized, mocked, and eventually arrested. His death was one of sacrifice. Compassion, faithfulness, and sacrifice are hard choices to make. It can take a whole lifetime to do it well, but we can start now. We can be compassionate. We can be faithful. We can make sacrifices. We can look for the dying and the rising in our own lives.

Something to Do

Use this space to tell why each of these situations is like dying and rising.

1. You shut off your favorite TV show to help your little sister with her building blocks.

_____

_____

_____

_____

2. You let your brother have the last doughnut, even though it's your favorite kind.

_____

_____

_____

3. Describe a situation in which you might need to put on the compassion of Jesus.

_____

_____

_____

4. Describe a situation in which you might need the courage and faithfulness of Jesus.

_____

_____

_____

In Our Parish

- Which memorial acclamation is sung most often?
- Can you sing all the ones your parish knows?

LEARNING ABOUT
Liturgy

Liturgy of the Eucharist: Real Presence

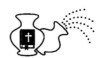

"This is my body … this is my blood."

—Mk 14:22;24

Our Lives

Amanda and Katie spent as much time together as they possibly could these days. They couldn't believe they would soon be separated. Amanda's mom was in the Air Force, and she was about to be stationed in Japan. Both girls were very unhappy knowing they were losing a good friend.

The day before her family had to leave, Amanda hung out with Katie for a long time. She wanted Katie to have something special to remember her by when she was gone, so Amanda gave Katie her favorite stuffed bear. "I want you to take the one I like the most," Amanda explained. "Then it will be like a part of me will always be with you."

Every time Katie held the stuffed bear, she felt close to Amanda, even though they were far away and wouldn't see each other for a long, long time.

Our Liturgy

When Jesus knew he was about to be arrested and crucified, he wanted to find a way to stay with his disciples forever. He wanted to give them a way to remember him that would last always. So when he was eating with his disciples for the last time, he did something unique. What he did is now the central action of our eucharistic liturgy (refer to Eucharistic Prayer III in the sacramentary):

This handout taken from *Learning about Liturgy,* © 2001 Dorothy Kosinski Carola. All rights reserved.

On the night he was betrayed,
he took bread and gave you thanks and praise.
He broke the bread, gave it to his disciples, and said:
Take this, all of you, and eat it:
this is my body which will be given up for you.

When supper was ended, he took the cup.
Again he gave you thanks and praise,
gave the cup to his disciples, and said:
Take this, all of you, and drink from it:
this is the cup of my blood,
the blood of the new and everlasting covenant.
It will be shed for you and for all
so that sins may be forgiven.
Do this in memory of me.

The bread and wine that we offered to God now becomes the Body and Blood of Jesus. The bread still tastes like bread, and the wine still tastes like wine, but Jesus is *really present* under the appearance of bread and wine. When we come to communion, the minister says "The Body of Christ" and "The Blood of Christ." Our "Amen" means that we believe it.

But those words have another meaning too. When we eat the Body of Christ, we *become* the Body of Christ. When we drink the cup of blessing, we drink the living spirit of Jesus. Not only is the bread and wine changed; we are changed. We are changed not just as individuals but as a community. We are *in communion* with all the people who are at Mass with us and with everyone who shares in communion anywhere in the world. We are all the Body of Christ.

When we come to communion, we should be able to share in both forms if we want to. We may also choose whether to have the minister of communion place the consecrated bread in our hands or on our tongue. The choice is ours. Once, Catholics considered themselves unworthy to touch the consecrated bread with their hands. But we know that our hands are just as worthy (or unworthy) as our tongue.

It is also okay to chew the consecrated bread when it is in your mouth. (Once, this was not permitted.) Jesus gave us food with which to remember him. We do Jesus a great honor when we eat the food and drink the drink as he directed.

Many Catholics now prefer to have the communion minister place the eucharistic bread in their hands and to drink from the cup as well. They experience this as a wonderful sign of doing what Jesus said: "Take and eat …. Take and drink …."

Because we believe that the bread and wine have become the Body and Blood of Jesus, we treat the consecrated bread and wine with great respect. If any eucharistic wine is left over, the ministers drink it. If any eucharistic bread is left over, it may be consumed or placed in the tabernacle. The eucharistic bread remains in the tabernacle in case someone who is ill or dying wants communion. The tabernacle is also a place people come to pray. People often pray before the tabernacle because the consecrated bread is still the presence of Jesus, even when Mass is over.

Because we believe that we continually become the Body of Christ every time we share in communion, we should treat each other with great respect. It makes no sense to be careful with the eucharist bread and wine and careless with each other! The reverence we show for the consecrated bread and wine must be a sign of the reverence we show for one another.

Something to Know

• **Consecration** — the part of the eucharistic prayer in which we remember and make present the words and actions of Jesus at the Last Supper.

• **Tabernacle** — a strong container in which we place the eucharistic bread when Mass is finished. The tabernacle is usually very beautiful. It may be located in a side area of the church or in a separate chapel.

• **Sanctuary lamp** — a candle or oil lamp which burns near the tabernacle (unless it is empty). The flame is a sign of the presence of Jesus.

• **Sacrarium** — a sink in the church sacristy with a special drainpipe that goes directly into the earth. It does not go into a sewer or septic system. When the dishes that contained the consecrated bread and wine are cleaned, any crumbs or drops go into the sacrarium. That way, the eucharistic elements get washed into the earth, which is sacred because God made it.

• **Chalice** — any cup from which we drink the eucharistic wine.

• **Ciborium** — any plate or cup that contains the eucharistic bread.

Living Our Liturgy

Through communion, we are united with all the friends of Jesus all over the world. Some members of the Body of Christ have trouble learning to read. Some members of the Body of Christ have no one to play with in the school yard. Some members of the Body of Christ live in your house and need a kind word from you!

Some members of the Body of Christ need help learning English when they come to this country. Some members of the Body of Christ can't walk or hear or see. Some members of the Body of Christ can't afford to go to a doctor when they are sick. Some members of the Body of Christ are starving. Some members of the Body of Christ have no home to go to. Some members of the Body of Christ are at war. Some members of the Body of Christ are killed for helping the poor.

Something to Do

You are a member of the Body of Christ. Talk with your folks about how we should treat one another. Talk with your folks about how life could be more fair for more people.

After you talk it over, write down some of the ideas you had:

_____

_____

_____

_____

_____

In Our Parish

- Be sure you can identify the tabernacle and sanctuary lamp in your church.

- Does your parish offer communion in both forms?

- Ask the liturgy coordinator, priest, or a communion minister to show you the sacrarium, a chalice, and a ciborium.

- What are some of the programs, activities, works of charity, or works of justice your parish is involved in? How do these help life to be more fair for more people? Are there any *you* can help with?

_____

Notes

This handout taken from
Learning about Liturgy,
© 2001 Dorothy Kosinski Carola.
All rights reserved.

LEARNING ABOUT
Liturgy

Liturgy of the Eucharist: Looking Forward

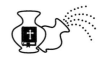

"Your Kingdom come. Your will be done on earth as it is in heaven."

—Mt 6:10

Our Lives

On Memorial Day, the Carnelli family held their usual family barbeque. The following week, they squeezed in their first trip to the town pool. Angelo and his brother, Vinnie, were very excited as the family began to plan their summer trip to Colorado. And it was great having extra daylight time to play with their friends after their homework was finished.

One afternoon, Angelo walked home from school with his friends. He told them how much he was looking forward to summer vacation. "You know, I'm so excited about summer, I'm getting restless with school. I know we still have school for another month, but it feels as if summer has already started. All I want to do are summer things, not school things!"

Our Liturgy

When we go to Mass, we are like Angelo looking forward to summer. Angelo could see that summer was near, and could already do some summer activities. When we go to Mass, we can see that the kingdom of God is near, and we can already do some of the kingdom activities. It felt like summer for Angelo, even though school was not over yet. When we go to Mass, it feels as if heaven is here, even though we're not there yet. Angelo felt as if summer was pulling him away from school and toward fun. At Mass, we are being pulled toward the kingdom and away from the world's sinful ways. It's kind of a funny feeling for heaven to be here

This handout taken from
Learning about Liturgy,
© 2001 Dorothy Kosinski Carola.
All rights reserved.

63

now, but not here at the same time.

In the Liturgy of the Eucharist, not only do we remember and make present again the sacrifice of Jesus, we also look forward. We look forward to being better people because of our participation in the Eucharist. We look forward to Jesus' coming again at the end of time. We look forward to the fulfillment of God's kingdom.

In the Liturgy of the Eucharist, our looking forward is more than just wishing for something that hasn't happened yet. In the Eucharist, we touch what we hope for. God's people are drawn into the life of the Spirit just as Angelo was being drawn into the fun of summer. At Mass, heaven and earth meet.

This "looking forward" is woven into our worship during the Liturgy of the Eucharist. Listen to how we pray (you can find these prayers in the sacramentary):

Your gift of the Spirit,
who raised Jesus from the dead,
is the foretaste and promise
of the paschal feast of heaven (*Preface 34*).

Father,
in this eucharist
we touch the divine life you give to the world.
Help us to follow Christ with love
to eternal life where he is Lord for ever and ever
(*Prayer after Communion, Ascension*).

Merciful Father,
may these mysteries
give us new purpose
and bring us to a new life in you
(*Prayer after Communion, 16th Sunday in Ordinary Time*).

Lord Jesus Christ,
you give us your body and blood in the eucharist
as a sign that even now we share your life.
May we come to possess it completely in the kingdom
where you live for ever and ever
(*Prayer after Communion, Body and Blood of Christ*).

These are just a few examples of the prayers that help us focus on looking forward. In the liturgy, we can see what is waiting for those who live their baptismal call. We can see the shape of the world to come, of the kingdom God desires, and of the people God wants us to be.

Living Our Liturgy

People who can imagine what they cannot completely see live and act differently. Christopher Columbus could envision a round earth, so he sailed west to get to the East. This seemed backward to most people, but now we know it wasn't. At liturgy, we don't just imagine the kingdom of God, we taste it and see it. This can lead us to some "strange" behavior too. It can lead us to treat everyone fairly. It can lead us to help the poor lead better lives. It can lead us to put aside violent ways for peaceful ways. When Christopher Columbus got to the Americas, people found out that his choice was not so odd after all. When God's kingdom comes in its fullness, everyone will find out that the Christian way is not so odd either. In fact, it's exactly what God has in mind.

Something to Do

On drawing paper, show how you envision the kingdom of God.

In Our Parish

What helps you taste and see the kingdom of God at liturgy?

This handout taken from
Learning about Liturgy,
© 2001 Dorothy Kosinski Carola.
All rights reserved.

LEARNING ABOUT
Liturgy

Lesson 16 Handout

Concluding Rite

Our Lives

"When will that game be finished, Luisa? You need to start your homework," Teresa called to her younger sister. "I just got to the next level," Luisa answered as she pushed the buttons on her electronic game. "But when will it be finished?" Teresa persisted.

"Well, it's never really finished," Luisa explained. "You just keep going to the next level. But I'll start my homework when this level is done."

Teresa examined the game as Luisa got out her homework papers. "How many levels does this thing have?" she asked. "I'm not sure," Luisa answered. "I didn't get to all of them yet."

Our Liturgy

When is the liturgy finished? Once the communion rite is over, we are nearly ready to leave. But, like Luisa's electronic game, the liturgy is never really finished. There are many levels yet to come, and it could take awhile before we get to all of them.

The Concluding Rite is short, but it still has a most important role in the liturgy. Following the prayer after communion, there may be some announcements about events that are happening in the parish. This is a good way to let people know what's going on. There are often many parish activities that need our help or that can be helpful to us.

Next, the priest offers a blessing. It may be short:

May almighty God bless you,
the Father, and the Son, and the Holy Spirit. (*Amen.*)

Or it may be longer:

"No one after lighting a lamp puts it under the bushel basket, but on the lampstand, and it gives light to all in the house. In the same way, let your light shine before others, so that they may see your good works and give glory to your Father in heaven."

—Mt 5:15–16

May almighty God keep you from all harm
and bless you with every good gift. (*Amen.*)
May he set his Word in your heart
and fill you with lasting joy. (*Amen.*)
May you walk always in his ways,
always knowing what is right and good,
until you enter your heavenly inheritance. (*Amen.*)
(*Solemn Blessing, Ordinary Time V*)

After the blessing, the deacon or the priest dismisses us. He may say:

Go in the peace of Christ.

or

The Mass is ended, go in peace.

or

Go in peace to love and serve the Lord.

We answer: "*Thanks be to God.*"

It is interesting that we often call our liturgy "the Mass." The word "Mass" comes from the word "dismissal." This tells us so much about why we come for liturgy. We gather at the church to be dismissed. The dismissal sends us forth to do good works, to make Christ known by the way we live. In an earlier time in church history, the dismissal was the longest part of the liturgy! Every person present would come forward for an individual blessing and dismissal by the bishop.

The dismissal tells us that the reason we leave is just as important as the reason we come. Having been nourished by God's word and sacrament, we are dismissed to live this way of grace everywhere we go.

It may be time to leave the church, but, in a way, the liturgy is never concluded. Just as we get ready for Mass before we actually arrive at the church, the dismissal sends us back to our homes, to our schools, to our jobs, and to our neighborhoods to continue what began at liturgy. It is up to us to take the liturgy to the next level.

Living Our Liturgy

If we take the word of God and the Body and Blood of Christ into our hearts week by week, we will be transformed. Our hearts will turn away from whatever hurts people and turn toward all that brings people hope and help. This is the conversion that liturgy is all about. It takes a lifetime, but it happens continually as we give ourselves to the great prayer of the church.

Something to Do

In this space, write down some ways that you "let your light shine before others."

_____

_____

_____

_____

_____

_____

In Our Parish

What activities does your parish sponsor that helps people take liturgy "to the next level"? Look for activities that extend Jesus' care to those outside the parish. Are there any in which you could participate?

_____

Notes

LEARNING ABOUT Liturgy

Lesson 17 Handout

Sunday Celebrations in the Absence of a Priest

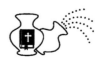

"All who believed were together."

—Acts 2:44

Our Lives

"I don't even want to go if Uncle Jack won't be there!" Christopher complained. "He's always the most fun!" "But we always have Easter dinner at Aunt Eileen's house, and your cousins are looking forward to seeing you," Mom explained. "Besides, Aunt Eileen will really need the company if Uncle Jack can't get home in time. Don't you think she will miss him even more than you will?"

"I guess so," Christopher answered. "But he always brings the coolest stuff from his trips across the country. Why did he have to get stuck in that snow storm in Maine anyway?" "That was just bad luck," Mom continued. "I know it won't be the same, but even without Uncle Jack, we have Easter to celebrate, and family to enjoy. I bet you'll have a good time anyway."

Our Liturgy

In many areas of our country today, there are not enough priests to celebrate the liturgy in all the churches where Catholics gather. Sometimes, Catholics must travel longer distances to get to Mass. Sometimes, priests travel from one parish to another to preside at Mass for the people. Sometimes, there is no priest to send to a particular church, so the people there cannot participate in the liturgy on Sunday at all. When this happens, the people may

This handout taken from *Learning about Liturgy,* © 2001 Dorothy Kosinski Carola. All rights reserved.

gather for a communion service instead.

Even when a priest cannot be there, the church wants the believers to gather for prayer and Scripture. This tells us how important the gathering of the assembly really is. Believers need to be with each other to pray even when there is no priest. They share in communion that was consecrated at a Mass held earlier or at a Mass held somewhere else. Although it is sad that the assembly cannot participate in the Mass, believers always have their faith to celebrate and the support of their community to enjoy.

A communion service is led by a person who is not a priest. It may include the Liturgy of the Hours, either Morning Prayer or Evening Prayer. It may include the Liturgy of the Word, just as at Mass. It does *not* include the Liturgy of the Eucharist because only a priest can preside over the eucharistic prayer. We do not bring our gifts of bread and wine to be consecrated. The sacrifice of Jesus is not made present again. When we share in communion, it can only be offered in the form of bread because we usually do not reserve the sacrament in the form of wine. But we do share the Body of Christ consecrated at another Mass at which other Catholics were present and praying for us. In this way, a communion service emphasizes the oneness of all believers.

A communion service is not the ideal way for Catholics to celebrate the Lord's day. Still, the communion service can help us focus on the other ways Jesus is present to us. We can discover new ways of being church.

Jesus is always present in the gathered assembly. Jesus has assured us that "where two or three are gathered in my name, I am there among them" (Mt 18:20). Whether it's Mass or not, the assembly is always the most important minister at liturgy. It is the assembly who prays and who lifts each other's prayers to God. When there is no Mass, we might see even better how important we are to one another. Perhaps we can take this opportunity to get to know people in our assembly better.

We can discover how lay people serve and support one another in the church. When there is no priest, lay people will often plan, prepare, and lead the communion service. This helps us to be aware of the important role lay people play in the church. Lay people can find new church ministries and roles of leadership in which they can use their talents for the good of the church.

We can discover that our Sunday celebration is still the most important way for us to experience the healing and support that keeps our faith going. When we are not able to participate in Mass, we might appreciate it even more.

When we participate in a communion service, we are taking our role as church very seriously. The church is the community of believers, not the priest alone. We are church for each other. Just as Christopher's aunt needed his company, we need the company of other believers. We have the Lord's Day to celebrate even if there is no priest.

Living Our Liturgy

When we participate in a communion service, we strengthen one another through our prayer. Each day, pray for your assembly. Pray for your church. Pray that we will see God's guidance as we try to be the Catholic Church even when there is no Eucharist to celebrate.

Something to Do

Use the diagram on the next page to show the differences and similarities between Mass and a Sunday celebration without a priest.

In Our Parish

• Is Mass celebrated every weekend in your parish, or do you sometimes celebrate a communion service? If you celebrate a communion service, who prepares it? Who leads it?

• For parishes that regularly celebrate Sunday Eucharist: What if you went to church next weekend and found that no priest could be there? What would people do? How would you pray? Who would decide? Who would lead?

Notes

This handout taken from
Learning about Liturgy,
© 2001 Dorothy Kosinski Carola.
All rights reserved.

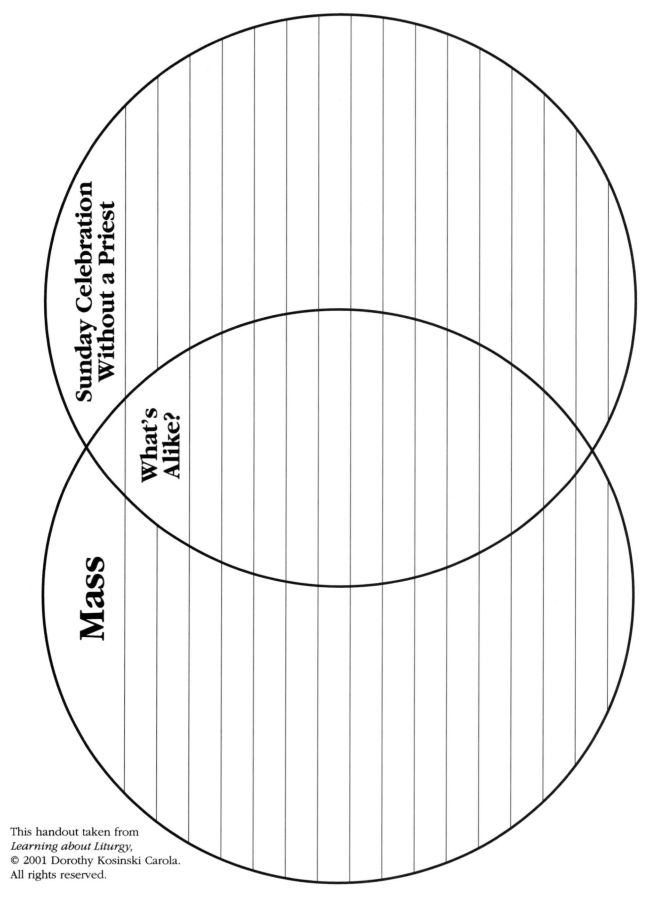

Sunday Celebration
Without a Priest

What's
Alike?

Mass

This handout taken from
Learning about Liturgy,
© 2001 Dorothy Kosinski Carola.
All rights reserved.

Part 2

Lesson Plans

What Is Liturgy? #1

Objectives

- To understand liturgy as formative of our faith and spirituality.

- To provide a model for understanding liturgy.

- To encourage regular attendance at liturgy.

Preparation

- Read Lessons 1 and 2 and their handouts in advance.

- The first two lessons can be used together if time and your group structure allow. Determine whether you will use these lessons together in one meeting or in separate meetings.

- If there is a potter in your area, you may be able to arrange for your group to visit him or her to experience firsthand the image of liturgy being presented in these first two lessons.

- For Prayer Option I, if you do not already know it, learn the song "Abba, Father" by Carey Landry (North American Liturgy Resources, 1977), or secure a recording of it.

Supplies

- Sufficient copies of Lesson 1 Handout

- Sufficient pens or pencils

- Sufficient Bibles

- Any children's modeling clay that *air-dries*

- *Optional:* audio equipment and a recording of "Abba, Father" by Carey Landry

Background

People come to liturgy with a wide variety of expectations. For some, liturgy is "good" if they feel exhilarated, a "spiritual high." For others, liturgy is "good" if they feel calmed and at peace. Others will call it "good" if they laughed; still others call it "good" if the choir or ensemble offered beautiful music. Others will expect to "learn something" from a scholarly homily. It is easy to see how a single liturgy could hardly bear the weight of all these expectations.

The purpose of the two opening lessons is to present a model for thinking about the role of liturgy in the lives of Catholics. Liturgy is, first and foremost, prayer. The purpose of prayer is not so much to produce particular feelings, to entertain, or to teach. Rather, it is to draw us further and further into the life of God, to form us, individually and communally, into God's people.

The image of pottery-making was chosen to highlight this formational effect of liturgy. Both from the second Genesis story of creation (cf. Gn 2:4–7) and from Jeremiah's imagery (cf. Jer 18:6), we connect easily to the picture of ourselves as clay and God as the one who shapes the clay. With God as the potter, we should have no trouble giving ourselves over to the process. This, then, is all we need to expect from liturgy: If we give ourselves over to the process, we *will* be shaped and formed into earthen vessels that overflow with God's grace.

Introducing the Topic

If your group is unfamiliar with the word "liturgy," you may want to begin with the Something to Know section.

Talk with your group to discover whether they are familiar with how a potter works. Use this as a jumping-off point for this lesson.

The Scripture

Read aloud the Scripture quotation. Ask your group to share about why the prophet Jeremiah might compare us to clay and God to a potter. (God is our maker; God created us out of clay; God is always shaping us; God's hands are always getting messy trying to mold us.)

Our Lives

Have your group read this section aloud or silently. Talk with them about how a potter works. The essential ingredients are clay that is moist enough but not too wet, and therefore formable; the constantly spinning pottery wheel; the centering of the clay on the wheel for a piece that is balanced; the skilled hands of the potter. If you are able to visit or speak with a potter, he or she could best describe or demonstrate the process.

During this discussion, you might work a piece of children's modeling clay in your hands. If you can form it into something recognizable, like a person or a church, or a bowl or a vase, so much the better. If you cannot, it will suffice to simply squeeze and knead the clay as the lesson progresses. This doesn't really come close to demonstrating pottery-making, but it will impress on the group the shaping and forming that goes on at liturgy. It will also allow you to demonstrate what happens when the clay is left out.

Our Liturgy

Have your group read this section aloud or silently. Probe their understanding of it with questions like these:

- **What are some of the ways God is active in your life?** *(People may recount some personal experience of God; they may speak of the gifts they have been given; accept all reasonable responses.)*

- Why do we say that liturgy is like pottery-making? *(Mass is an important way God is active in our lives; God shapes and forms us through liturgy; God is forming a people; liturgy is like God's pottery wheel.)*

- **What do we do at Mass that helps to form and mold us?** *(Accept answers given in the final paragraph of this section, or responses from the group's own experience of liturgy.)*

Something to Know

Review the information provided here. Explain that, although there are other kinds of liturgy besides Mass (namely, the other sacraments and the Liturgy of the Hours), we will use the two words interchangeably in *Learning about Liturgy.*

Allow your group to offer their thoughts about why our public worship might have come to be named after the *last* thing that happens—the dismissal. (This tells us that the sending forth is a pretty important aspect of what Mass is about. In the dismissal we are sent forth to live the Gospel life we have just celebrated and in which we have just been nourished. This is discussed further in Lesson 16.)

Living Our Liturgy

If you have been working a piece of clay, choose a shape to leave it in. (A lump will do.) Ask the group what will happen to that clay if it is left out. (It will become dry and hard.) If your meeting space will permit, leave the clay until your next meeting. If not, take it with you and bring it back to the next meeting. Keep some fresh clay and the hard clay on hand as a reminder of which kind of clay we want to be, and as a reminder to participate in Sunday liturgy.

Have the group read this section aloud or silently. Be sure they understand the comparison between clay that's left out and leaving themselves out of Mass.

In working with children, be aware that their attendance at Mass is usually not their choice. Do not berate them for nonattendance, but suggest they discuss some of their responses to the Something to Do activity with the adults who *are* responsible for this decision in their household.

Something to Do

Allow your group time to complete this section. Those who wish may share their responses.

Prayer Experience

- *Option I:* Gather your group in a prayer center or in a circle. Help your group learn, if they do not already know, the song "Abba, Father" by Carey Landry. While especially appropriate for the first two lessons, this song can be used effectively for prayer at any time throughout the program.

- *Option II:* Pray Psalm 100 together with your group. If the group is large enough, divide the group in two and alternate verses.

What Is Liturgy? #2

Objectives

- To further explore the pottery model as a way of understanding liturgy.

- To provide a second model for understanding liturgy.

- To appreciate how God acts in our lives through liturgy.

Preparation

- Read Lessons 1 and 2 and their handouts in advance.

- Determine whether you will use these lessons in one session or two.

- *Optional*: A printed or audio resource containing the song "Earthen Vessels" by John B. Foley, SJ (New Dawn Music, 1975).

Supplies

- Sufficient copies of Lesson 2 Handout

- Sufficient pens or pencil

- Drawing supplies

- If possible, a pottery jar or pitcher filled with water

- If possible, a water sprinkler such as that used in church during the sprinkling rite, an evergreen branch, or whatever your parish uses for the rite of sprinkling

- *Optional:* audio equipment to play the song "Earthen Vessels"

Background

God's action in our lives is never given for our own sake alone, but for the sake of the world's transformation into God's kingdom. As our Christian lives are given shape by the liturgy, so too are they filled with the life of Jesus. This, then, provides the second image we will use to understand the role of liturgy in our lives: liturgy as a fountain of God's life and grace. The shaping and forming that happens at liturgy is meant to make us vessels of God's grace. It is not enough, however, for us to be filled up and feeling good about it—cozy and content with Jesus. Only when our vessel is overflowing, being emptied out, or even just cracked and leaking, can the world be awash in God's grace.

Introducing the Topic

Display the water-filled pottery vessel in your meeting place without comment.

Open your session by singing "Abba, Father." Ask your group to describe why this song is appropriate to your lessons about liturgy. (Liturgy is God's way of molding and shaping us.)

Use this as your jumping-off point for this lesson.

The Scripture

Have a member of the group read the Scripture quotation aloud. Allow them to share their ideas about its meaning in the context of these two lessons. Stimulate discussion by asking questions such as these:

- **Who are the "clay jars" St. Paul is talking about?** (*We are; St. Paul is comparing us to clay jars that are filled with the life of God; a clay jar is a humble vessel for so great a power, so people will be able to tell that what they see is God's life in us.*)

- **What treasure do these clay jars hold?** (*The glory of Jesus; the power of God.*)

Our Lives

Have your group read the opening story aloud or silently. Explore the meaning of the story by asking why the girls didn't want the vase to remain empty. (That's not what vases are for; they wanted Grandma to use the gift they gave her.)

Our Liturgy

Read the section aloud or silently. Delve into this section with questions like these:

- **Why can we say liturgy is also like a fountain?** (*God's grace is being poured out for us in a special way at liturgy.*)

- **So why is God molding and shaping us?** (*We'll be like clay jars that are filled with the life of God.*)

- **Why should we be filled with the life of God?** (*so that we're not empty; so that we fulfill God's purpose in shaping us in the first place; so that God's life can flow through us and pour out of us into the lives of others.*)

This may be a good point at which to refer back to Lesson 1, in which we learned that the word "Mass" comes from "dismissal." We wondered why the liturgy would be named for the last thing that happens. Now we can see how the going forth is very much at the heart of it all. We come to be filled with the life of God so that it can flow through us to the rest of the world. In other words, this end result is really what it's all about.

Something to Know

Review the information in this section. Help the group understand that these are the four *principal* parts of the liturgy. Throughout the program, you will find out about many more elements that make up each of these four parts.

Living Our Liturgy

After reading this section, lead your group in a discussion prompted by the questions that end the section.

Activity: Using the drawing supplies you provide, have your group depict an "earthen vessel" or a "clay jar" being filled with God's life that flows out to others.

Something to Do

It may be possible for your group to complete this section just from their experience of liturgy, but it would be more engaging to assign it as "homework" to be completed after they next attend Mass. Remember to begin your next session by reviewing this section.

Prayer Experience

- Gather your group in a prayer center, or in a circle.

- Use your voice or a recording to lead your group in singing "Earthen Vessels."

- If possible, use the water sprinkler to bless them with the water, *or* let them each dip their hand in the water and bless one another with a sign of the cross on the forehead. Conclude with a prayer like this:

Gracious God, fill us with your life,
so that when we pour ourselves out for others,
all who need you will know your love.
We ask this through Christ our Lord.

Introductory Rites

Objectives

- To understand the role of the Introductory Rites in the liturgy.

- To appreciate the need to prepare well for Mass.

- To appreciate Sunday as a day of rest.

Preparation

- Read Lesson 3 and its handout in advance.

- *Optional:* Know where to find the prayers and responses of the Introductory Rites in your parish worship aid.

- Be able to lead your group in singing a "Gloria" sung in your parish, or recruit someone who can.

- Collect the information you will need to guide your group through the In Our Parish section.

Supplies

- Sufficient copies of Lesson 3 Handout

- Sufficient pens or pencils

- *Optional:* copies of your parish worship aid

- *Optional:* sufficient copies of the After-Mass Worksheet

Background

Preparing to celebrate Jesus in word and sacrament has both a ritual and a nonritual component. Within the liturgy, the Introductory Rites serve to prepare us, to open us up, to whatever God wants to do or say in our lives that day. We don't jump right into the Liturgy of the Word. We get ready. We hope that this getting ready happens before we arrive. The time we set aside for Mass should be more than the time actually spent in church. This way, the liturgy can be much more fruitful in our lives. When it is just the hour we stop at church, in between Johnny's ball game and the trip to the grocery store, something is lost. Contemporary lifestyles make a true sabbath rest difficult for some and impossible for others. Nonetheless, keeping it as a goal ensures that some of us will achieve something like it once in a while. Some stress-free, unscheduled time before and after Mass is a good step in the right direction. Some may want to use that time for prayer or Scripture reading.

The informal preparation for liturgy takes on another form as we begin to gather at the church. With or without official greeters, everyone who gathers has a responsibility for hospitality. The way we greet one another sets a tone that should make worship possible. By seeking out newcomers, and with conversation, we express our pleasure at being together. Our demeanor and our approach to others in the assembly generates an openness and a welcoming atmosphere that helps those gathered open up to God's action in their lives.

In such a welcoming atmosphere, the ritual components of getting ready can be that much more effective. The unitive power of the opening song affirms and amplifies what has been taking place in our gathering. As we plunge into the prayer and praise of the Introductory Rites, our hardened hearts are softened like tilled earth to receive the fertile seed of God's word and sacrament.

Introducing the Topic

Find out if your group is aware of how we get ready once the Mass has begun. Ask them to name some of the parts of the Mass that help us get ready to celebrate the liturgy. *(Any components of the Introductory Rites can be mentioned here.)*

The Scripture

Have someone read aloud the Scripture quotation. Remind the group that you will be examining the beginning parts of the Mass that help us prepare for the Liturgy of the Word and the Liturgy of the Eucharist.

Our Lives

Have your group read the story aloud or silently. Ask them to mention some special events with which they are familiar. Ask what kind of preparations need to be made for those events. (Accept all reasonable responses.)

Our Liturgy

Have your group read the first four paragraphs of this section, which discuss the preparation for liturgy that we do at home. Explore their understanding with questions like these:

- **What are some of the ways you get ready for Mass?** *(Accept all reasonable responses; focus especially on those that seem to indicate that Sunday is a special day unlike the rest of the week.)*

- **Why are we expected not to eat for one hour before Mass?** *(This is a way of preparing; we want to be hungry for God; fasting from regular food helps us focus on the sacred food we will receive at Mass.)*

- **Imagine you could go up in a helicopter and watch everyone coming to church. Can you picture all the People of God on their way to church from all of their homes?** *(Give them a moment to picture it.)* **Wouldn't it look like a big procession?**

(Comment that each person in that procession is answering God's invitation to be at church with God's people.)

Have your group read the next paragraph. Discuss with them how people are made to feel welcome in your parish.

Read the section describing the formal Introductory Rites. Ask your group to name other examples of singing that unites people. (The national anthem at a sports event; camp groups around a campfire; singing Christmas carols at a Christmas party.)

Have your group practice the response to the priest's greeting.

Ask you group to consider the meaning of the penitential rite. For example, why do we look at our sins and ask God's mercy as a way of getting ready? (This is a moment in which we express our need for God's help in our lives; remembering that we need God's help makes us ready to hear God's word.)

Something to Know

Review the information in this section.

Optional: Using copies of your parish worship aid, have the group practice the prayers and responses that are part of the Introductory Rites. Suggest to them that the goal is to memorize these passages so we can pray them from our hearts.

Living Our Liturgy

After reading the section, ask your group to brainstorm some situations in which being ready to listen to God and being close to God's people would make Christian living easier. (Accept all reasonable answers. Responses could focus on moments of temptation when openness to God keeps us safe or keeps us on the right path; or on moments of peer pressure when knowing other Christians are living like you gives you courage and encouragement.)

Something to Do

Allow your group time to respond to and share their responses to the questions in this section. (Accept all reasonable responses.)

In Our Parish

Guide your group through this section using the information you gathered in advance.

Prayer Experience

Gather your group in a prayer center, or in a circle. Sing a "Gloria" used in your parish.

Liturgy of the Word: Overview

Objectives

- To appreciate listening and responding as the primary activities of the Liturgy of the Word.

- To understand what it takes to listen well.

- To know the parts of the Liturgy of the Word.

Preparation

- Read Lesson 4 and its handout in advance.

- Do whatever research is necessary to guide your group through the In Our Parish section.

- Be sure you can find each section of the Bible from which the Scripture readings are taken so you can point them out to your group.

- *Optional:* Prepare five copies of Lesson 4 Handout and highlight the spoken parts of the opening story according to the speaker. For instance, on one copy highlight Marc's words, on another Jamal's words, Dad's words on the third copy, and Mom's words on the fourth copy. On the fifth copy, highlight any words *not* in quotation marks for the narrator. Distribute these copies to different members of your group. Allow them to tell the story with different speakers in each role. This will be even more effective if they have time to prepare in advance of the session.

- *Optional:* Be prepared to teach a song from your parish repertoire about listening to and following God's word. Ask your music director for assistance in making the selection, or consider these possibilities:

"Speak, Lord" by Marienne Uszler and Tim Schoenbachler (OCP Publications, 1979)

"The Good News of God's Salvation" by Christopher Walker (OCP Publications, 1988)

Supplies

- Sufficient copies of Lesson 4 Handout

- Sufficient Bibles

- Sufficient pens or pencils

- *Optional:* five copies of the handout with each speaker's part in the Our Lives section highlighted
- *Optional:* drawing supplies
- *Optional:* writing paper
- *Optional:* the Scripture citations for the coming Sunday or a resource containing the Sunday Scriptures
- *Optional:* sufficient After-Mass Worksheets for your group

Background

The Liturgy of the Word constitutes the first half of the Mass. It is the complement of the Liturgy of the Eucharist and is inseparable from it. We are prepared to come to the table by the proclamation of the word. The Scripture informs and sustains our Christian way of life just as the Eucharist does.

The word of God is proclaimed in the midst of the liturgical assembly for the sake of our formation as a people and for our continuing conversion to the ways of Christ. This makes it quite distinct from, for instance, Scripture study in a classroom or study group. This is not to say that knowledge cannot be gained at liturgy, nor that inspiration is necessarily absent from study groups. It is only to say that at liturgy, our primary purposes are not catechetical, and the kinds of activities appropriate in a catechetical setting will not be appropriate in a liturgical setting. (This distinction poses a constant challenge for those who prepare and preach at children's Liturgy of the Word services.) The purpose of proclamation at liturgy is conversion, furthering our life in the Spirit. This is why the assembly is expected to *listen* to the proclamations of Scripture and *not* read along with the proclaimer.

Those accustomed to reading along find this a difficult adjustment. Think of it this way: God is speaking to you. Wouldn't you want to drop everything and listen? If that means dropping a worship aid with printed Scriptures, so be it. Don't let anything come between you and God's word!

For a good example of what it means for the word of God to be proclaimed in our midst, spend some time with Nehemiah 8:1–13. Here we see a people whose hearts are captivated and enthralled by the word of God. Their tears flow freely, perhaps for sorrow at how poorly they have lived the covenant, perhaps for joy at how generous God has been. In any regard, it is clear that they did not gather for any mere Scripture lesson. That gathering reaffirmed their life as God's people and sent them out feasting and rejoicing and sharing what they had. Would that the proclamation of God's word at liturgy so moved us!

Introducing the Topic

Ask your group what they know about the Liturgy of the Word. Use their responses as a lead-in to Lesson 4.

The Scripture

Have someone read aloud the Scripture that begins this lesson. Allow them to offer their insights into what this short line of Scripture is trying to tell us. (Responses may focus on these or similar ideas: God's word is not just ancient history; it's about us. God's word can have an effect on us and how we live; God's word can change us.)

 ## Our Lives

Have your group read the opening story aloud or silently.

Optional: For best effect, have members take the roles of the different characters in the story, using the highlighted pages you prepared in advance.

Probe the meaning of the story with questions like these:

- **Who in this story really listened to Marc?** *(Mom)*

- **How could Marc tell that Jamal wasn't listening?** *(Jamal went on to a totally different topic and couldn't even tell how Marc was feeling.)*

- **How could Marc tell his dad wasn't listening?** *(His dad heard what he said, but he was too busy with his own work to pay good attention to Marc. He just sort of brushed him off and didn't let him get his point across.)*

- **How could Marc tell that his mom was listening?** *(She stopped what she was doing and looked at him while he spoke.)*

- **Why didn't Marc keep the conversation going with Jamal or his dad?** *(He could tell from the response he got that they weren't really paying attention to him.)*

- **Has anything like this ever happened to you? How did it feel?** *(Accept all reasonable responses.)*

Our Liturgy

Allow your group to read the first two paragraphs aloud or silently.

Be sure your group understands what it means to say that the living God is speaking through God's word at liturgy. (God's will for us is communicated when the word is proclaimed; Jesus' presence is not only in the consecrated bread and wine, but in the speaking of the word by the lector and priest or deacon; When God's word is proclaimed, it is the voice and person of the lector or priest that allows God's presence to be heard. God is present in the proclamation, not in the ink on the page.)

Have your group read the remainder of the section aloud or silently. Check for content comprehension with questions like these:

- **What's the best way to absorb the word of God when it is proclaimed at Mass?** *(By listening attentively.)*

- **Name two ways that responding is built in to the Liturgy of the Word.** *(Through the silences that follow the readings and the homily; in the singing of the psalm.)*

- **What postures do we use during the Liturgy of the Word? How do these help us?** *(Sitting helps us be relaxed and open; standing for the Gospel helps us pay special attention.)*

Optional: Distribute drawing paper and a coloring medium. Ask each member of your group to depict *listening* and *responding,* either in one drawing or in two, one on each half of the page. Allow time for members to share and describe their drawings. Suggest that they use these drawings as reminders of what is expected of them during the Liturgy of the Word.

Something to Know

Review the information in this section. Have members of your group describe what they see and do for each of these elements of the Liturgy of the Word.

Living Our Liturgy

After your group has read this section, have them make a list, either orally or in writing, of the ways in which they respond to the word of God in their lives.

Something to Do

Provide your group with the citations of the Scripture readings for the *coming* weekend so that they can complete the activity suggested in the first part of this section. If time permits, read the Scriptures together. If time does not permit, suggest that they read them at home. Let them know that you will revisit this question in several weeks when everyone has had a chance to listen carefully at Mass. (The After-Mass Worksheet may be helpful in allowing the group to keep track of their reactions.)

In Our Parish

- If a large Bible or Book of Gospels is on display in the church, describe it for the group, and suggest that they identify it the next time they are in church. (If circumstances permit, you might go see the display.) Talk with them about what such a display means. (That the word of God is very important to us; that Jesus isn't just in the tabernacle, but in the Scriptures too; that the word and the Eucharist are the two most important ways to feed our faith.)

- Ask the group to do this research and report back at your next session. Be sure to pick up with this when you begin your next session. (Possible responses: If your group reports that the silences are very short or nonexistent, they could be surprised because the silences are meant to be longer and an important element of listening and responding may not be getting the attention it deserves. If your group reports that the silences *seem* long, they might be surprised to learn that the quiet time is really only ten or twenty or thirty seconds. [If your parish routinely holds silences longer than thirty seconds, count your blessings and congratulate your presiders.] If your group reports that the silences *do not seem* long, it could be because they are too short, or because your assembly has grown blessedly accustomed to significant silences.)

Prayer Experience

- *Option I:* Teach the song "Speak, Lord," "When We Hear God's Word," or a similar selection from your parish repertoire. Use this song as your closing prayer. Consider using this song for prayer during any of the next five lessons focusing on the Liturgy of the Word.

- *Option II:* Gather your group in a prayer center, or in a circle. Allow a moment for a prayerful silence to fall upon the group. Suggest that they listen with their hearts to this passage from the Gospel of Matthew about how important it is to listen and respond to the word of God.

Everyone who hears these word of mine and acts on them will be like a wise man who built his house on rock. The rain fell, the floods came, and the winds blew and beat on that house, but it did not fall, because it had been founded on rock. And everyone who hears these words of mine and does not act on them will be like a foolish man who built his house on sand. The rain fell, the floods came, the winds blew and beat against the house and it fell—and great was its fall! (Mt 7:24–28).

Leader: To each of these invocations, please respond: *Fill our hearts with your word, O Lord.*

When we open the Scriptures …	*Fill our hearts with your word, O Lord.*
When we gather as your people …	*Fill our hearts with your word, O Lord.*
When you speak in our midst …	*Fill our hearts with your word, O Lord.*
When your word is proclaimed …	*Fill our hearts with your word, O Lord.*
When the storm winds blow …	*Fill our hearts with your word, O Lord.*

Leader: Living God, we want to hear your word
            and take it into our hearts.
        Give us listening ears and welcoming hearts
        so that our lives will be built on your word.
        We ask this in the name of Jesus the Lord.

All: Amen.

Liturgy of the Word: First Reading

Objectives

- To appreciate how the stories of our salvation are treasured by our tradition.

- To understand the role of the Old Testament reading in the Liturgy of the Word.

- To become familiar with some of the terms pertinent to the Liturgy of the Word.

Preparation

- Read Lesson 5 and its handout in advance.

- Find the Scripture citation for the first reading for the coming Sunday.

- Learn what you can about the design of the altar and ambo in your place of worship so you can guide your group through the In Our Parish section.

- If possible, arrange for a lector to speak with your group. Ask him or her to address the questions posed in the In Our Parish section. If this is not possible, plan to introduce yourselves to the lector after Mass this weekend.

Supplies

- Sufficient copies of Lesson 5 Handout

- Sufficient Bibles

- Sufficient pens or pencils

- *Optional:* Sufficient copies of the After-Mass Worksheet

Background

The first reading at liturgy is most often taken from the Old Testament. These are the first forty-five books of the Bible. Together with the New Testament, the Bible tells the story of salvation history.

To fully appreciate the Old Testament, it is helpful to realize that it contains a wide variety of literary forms. There are historical accounts, collections of advice, books of prophecy, eschatological writing (which looks toward the final days as a way to understand how to live our lives now), heroic stories, prayers, and much more. Page through your Bible to get a feel for the different kinds of literature there. Taken together, they unfold for us the great story of God's relationship with human beings, right from the beginning of time.

The Scriptures are the inspired word of God. This means that, although human authors chose the words, it is God's Spirit working through them that makes God known to us in what they have written. It does *not* mean that every word in the Bible is literally, historically, or scientifically factual. Truths of faith—not necessarily truths of history, astronomy, geography, and so forth—are revealed in the Bible. Understanding this will be of great help in knowing how to approach the Scripture readings, especially those from the Old Testament. We come to the Scriptures eager to know who God is, how God relates to people, and what God's will is for us. We will be distracted from this primary purpose if we come to Scripture trying to figure out who Cain and Abel married, precisely how the world began, how and when the world will end, or why people seemed to live so long in earlier days.

> All Scripture is inspired by God and is useful for teaching, for reproof, for correction, and for training in righteousness, so that everyone who belongs to God may be proficient, equipped for every good work (2 Tm 3:16).

During the Easter season, the first reading is taken from the Acts of the Apostles. This is appropriate, since the Easter season focuses so strongly on how the mission of Jesus is continued through his people. This book of the Bible shows us the growth of the early church and the spread of the faith from Jerusalem. We see how the apostles were challenged by the political powers, challenged to rethink their belief that Jesus' message was for Jewish people only, and challenged to live the life of justice that the Gospel demands.

Introducing the Topic

Elicit from your group what they already know about the first reading at Mass, and about the Old Testament. Use this to briefly describe the topic of this lesson.

The Scripture

Read aloud the Scripture that begins this lesson. Allow the group to share their understanding of it. (God is still speaking to us through the Bible. God's word is active because if we listen to it, God's word convinces us to do things we might not have done otherwise, like treat people fairly or share what we have with others)

Our Lives

Read the story aloud to your group, and then ask them to read the paragraph that follows. Check their understanding with questions like these:

- **Why do you think Jake wanted to hear his uncle's stories over and over again? (Because the stories helped him get to know his uncle; because they revealed to Jake something about his**

*family's history; because knowing about his elders'
childhood helped him relate to them better; because it was
fun to think about his elders as children.)*

- **Are there stories our/your family tells over and over? Perhaps
there's a story about when you were a baby, or a story about a
parent's childhood?** *(Allow them to share briefly.)*

Our Liturgy

Introduce this section by asking: What stories are important to
God's family? (The stories in the Bible.)

Have your group read this section aloud or silently. Direct your group's
reading of this section by suggesting they look for and share answers to the
following questions:

- **Where is the first reading at Mass taken from?** *(The first
reading is usually taken from the Old Testament; it is taken
from the Acts of the Apostles during the Easter season.)*

- **Why do we read stories about the Jewish people at Christian
worship?** *(The Jewish people were the first to know the true
God; God began offering salvation to us through the Jewish
people; the Christian story is a continuation of the Jewish
story.)*

Be sure your group understands that the first reading is intended to
connect with the Gospel reading in some way.

Optional: Examine the first reading and the Gospel for each of the
Sundays indicated. If your group is large enough, divide them into smaller
groups and assign one set of readings to each. Have them discuss or list on
paper how the two readings are connected:

- Fifth Sunday—Cycle A—Isaiah 58:7–10 and Matthew 5:13–16 *(Letting
the light of God shine in the good works you do.)*

- Ninth Sunday—Cycle B—Deuteronomy 5:12–15 and Mark 2:23—3:6
(What it really means to observe the sabbath.)

- Twenty-Second Sunday—Cycle C—Sirach 3:17–20,28–29 and Luke
14:1,7–14 *(Focus on humility.)*

Something to Know

Review the terms in this section. If circumstances permit, show
them the lectionary and the ambo in your place of worship, or have a lector
do so.

Living Our Liturgy

Refer back to the Scripture that began the lesson. Suggest to
your group that a good description of what this Scripture means is to be
found in the first paragraph of this section. Ask them to share a time when
they felt as if they really listened to the Scriptures, when the Scriptures
changed them, or when they felt God was speaking to them through a
specific Scripture. Be prepared to offer your own example as well.

Guide your group through the Something to Do section. Know in advance what Sunday of the year is coming up, what cycle it is, and find the appropriate citation for the first reading. They may read this passage from the Bibles you brought and complete the section alone, in groups, or as a do-at-home project.

In Our Parish

- If circumstances permit, visit your place of worship and point out the ambo. Otherwise, ask the group to find it on their next visit to church.

- Be prepared to point out similarities in design between the altar and the ambo, if they exist. (Often, these two main structures in the sanctuary are of similar design to emphasize the unity of the Liturgy of the Word and the Liturgy of the Eucharist. It is the proclamation of Scripture that prepares us to eat at the Lord's table. The fact that they look alike emphasizes the equal importance of the word and the sacrament.)

- Ask a lector to speak with your group about the nature and importance of this ministry, or plan to speak to the lector after Mass this weekend.

Prayer Experience

- Gather your group in a prayer center, or in a circle.

- Sing the song you taught in Lesson 4. Then proclaim Jeremiah 1:4–9. Conclude by blessing your group with this blessing from Numbers 6:24–26. Extend your right hand over the group as you say:

The Lord bless you and keep you;
The Lord make his face to shine upon you and be gracious to you;
The Lord lift up his countenance upon you and give you peace.

Liturgy of the Word: Psalm

Objectives

- To understand the role of the psalm in liturgy.

- To appreciate the psalms as sung scriptural prayers.

- To grow in appreciation of the psalms for use in private prayer.

Preparation

- Read Lesson 6 and its handout in advance.

- In a classroom or other group setting, try to arrange to have a parish cantor visit your class. Have the cantor speak about the meaning of the psalms, what it takes for him or her to prepare the psalms, what the role of psalmist means to him or her, and so on. This person would be the best candidate for answering the questions posed in the In Our Parish section. In a family setting, plan to introduce yourselves to the cantor after Mass. Thank him or her for being a psalmist. If time permits, you may want to ask similar questions.

- If this is not possible, do whatever research is necessary for you to provide the answers for the In Our Parish section of the lesson.

- *Optional Activity A:* Know what the first reading, psalm, and Gospel will be for the coming Sunday. If you need assistance, contact your parish liturgy coordinator, the person who administers *Learning about Liturgy*, or other parish personnel.

- *Optional Activity B:* Learn the psalm for the coming week. If you cannot sing it yourself, consider asking another member of the group to prepare it, use a recording, or ask the assistance of a parish cantor.

Supplies

- Sufficient copies of Lesson 6 Handout

- Sufficient pencils or pens

- *Optional:* sufficient Bibles for your group

- *Optional:* a resource providing the Scriptures and psalm for the coming Sunday

- *Optional:* an audio recording of the psalm for the coming Sunday, and equipment to play it

Background

There are 150 psalms found in the Book of Psalms in the Bible. The psalms are prayers preserved from Jewish worship many centuries before Jesus. Though the original Hebrew melodies are lost to us, we do know that the psalms were sung. Singing has always been a way to heighten the experience of prayer.

The role of the cantor in Jewish worship was, as it is today, taken very seriously. In the days before the psalms were written down, the cantor's song was the only way for people to become familiar with the psalms. Today, too, the cantor is the person chiefly responsible for proclaiming the psalms in the assembly. The document *Liturgical Music Today*, a 1982 statement of the American Bishop's Committee on the Liturgy, distinguishes the role of cantor from the role of psalmist. Although on a practical level, these two roles are often assigned to a single person, they are nonetheless distinct. This distinction highlights the fact that the psalm is *not* a "musical interlude" in the Liturgy of the Word. It is *not* just another of the hymns we sing at Mass. It is a proclamation of Scripture in song. The psalmist functions more like the lector during the Liturgy of the Word.

If you look at some of the psalms in the Bible, you will notice that lines expressing the same basic thought appear in pairs. This was an effective memory device used by the composers in the days before the psalms were written down. For example:

The law of the Lord is perfect, reviving the soul;
The decrees of the Lord are sure, making wise the simple

The precepts of the Lord are right, rejoicing the heart;
the commandment of the Lord is clear, enlightening the eyes;

The fear of the Lord is pure, enduring forever;
The ordinances of the Lord are true and righteous altogether.

More to be desired are they than gold; even much fine gold
sweeter also than honey, and the drippings of the honeycomb
(Ps 19:7–10).

In the Liturgy of the Word, the Mass gives us a model for our relationship with God. Our Catholic faith has long affirmed that it is God who takes the initiative in gathering a people together. We belong to God because God has sought us and called us. As God spoke to Noah, to Abraham and Sarah, and to Moses, as God spoke through Jesus, God speaks to us, and we respond. This is the pattern we find in the Liturgy of the Word. The ritual models this call-and-response by placing a sung psalm after the first reading. The psalm itself is proclaimed in call-and-response style. So when the cantor sings the psalm antiphon for all to repeat, then sings or speaks the verses between the antiphons, this is more than just an assembly-friendly way to proclaim the psalm. This is the pattern of our life with God.

Singing the psalm highlights and augments its proclamation. Singing has been an honored way of praying since ancient days. People have always confirmed through experience what we can now explain more scientifically: Music engages us in ways text alone cannot. Recent research has demonstrated that the two halves of the brain control different functions. The left side is associated primarily with logical, rational thinking (including language processing) and the right side with more intuitive, artistic endeavors (including music.) So, in fact, both halves of the brain are at work when we sing the psalm (or any prayer.) On our journey of faith, we cannot rely only on logical, rational thought. To do so would only get us halfway to God!

For the In Our Parish section, try to have a cantor, music director, or liturgy coordinator explain how the psalm is selected in your parish. If this person is unavailable, try to explain the process. The lectionary provides a specific psalm for each Sunday, which is chosen to complement the readings in some way. A number of music publishers provide musical settings for these *proper psalms*.

The lectionary also provides a set of *common psalms* for each season. These psalms complement the liturgical season well, and may be used for a number of weeks throughout a given season. This allows each community to decide whether its assembly will sing a new psalm every week, or whether they will learn to sing a few psalms well. As long as what is sung is actually a psalm, each community takes the responsibility for making this decision. Find out who makes that decision for your community and what the reasoning is behind it.

Introducing the Topic

Explain that today you will be exploring the psalms, and the use of psalms at Mass. Find out if anyone in your group already knows what psalms are, or what the responsorial psalm is at Mass. Use their responses as a lead-in to the materials in the handout.

The Scripture

Read aloud, or ask someone in your group to read aloud, the Scripture quote at the top of the page. Remind your group to consider this Scripture as they read today's lesson. At the end of the session, you will return to the Scripture to talk about its significance for this lesson.

Our Lives

Remind your group of their discussion of listening from Lesson 4 (Liturgy of the Word—Overview.) Talk again about how we can tell when another person is listening to us. Use examples from classroom or family life. Explain that this pattern of listening and responding will be found in the liturgy.

Our Liturgy

Read aloud or silently paragraphs 1 and 2. Ask the following questions:

- **Do you know when the psalm occurs in the Mass? (*Between the first and second readings.*)**

- **What is meant by the call-and-response form?** *(The cantor proclaims or "calls" the psalm verses and the people respond with the antiphon.)*

- **What does this form tell us about our relationship with God? *(God is calling us; God calls and we respond; when God speaks to us in the Scripture, God is waiting for us to answer.)***

- *Optional Activity A:* Share the first reading, the text of the psalm, and the Gospel reading for the coming Sunday with your group. Discuss how the psalm is related to the other two readings, especially the first. How does the psalm help us understand the other readings?

- *Optional Activity B:* If you have any facility with singing, if a recording of the psalm is available, or if a parish cantor is visiting your group, teach your group how to sing the antiphon of the psalm for the coming week. Have the group consider why singing the psalm is more effective than just proclaiming the words alone. *(An answer is offered in the next section of the text.)*

Read aloud or silently paragraphs 3 and 4. Allow the group to process the information with questions like these:

- **Did you know that the psalms were in the Bible?**

- **How does singing help us to pray the psalm?** *(By involving us more wholly; by engaging more of ourselves in the prayer.)*

- **What do you think St. Augustine meant when he said that "Those who sing, pray twice?"** *(He meant that the music and the words make a " double" prayer.)*

Activity: Distribute Bibles to your group. Have them look for the Book of Psalms. Ask them to find different kinds of psalms: Can they give an example of a psalm of praise, a psalm of sorrow, a psalm of thanksgiving, a psalm asking for help, a psalm of distress? Can they find a psalm for when a friend has made them angry? for when they are disappointed? for when they have succeeded? (Break down larger groups into smaller groups of two or three.) Read aloud some of the examples they find.

Read aloud or silently paragraph 5. Ask this question:

- **Why is the psalm sung from the same place as the Scriptures are read?** *(Because it's one of the Scripture proclamations, not just a song.)*

 # Something to Know

Review the information provided in this section.

Living Our Liturgy

Explain how people have used the psalms for private prayer as well as public worship for many centuries. Now that we know how many different kinds of psalms there are, it is easy to see why this is true.

Allow your group time to look over the psalms in the Living Our Liturgy section. Suggest to them that in their private prayer, they can pray one of these, or any other, psalms.

In Our Parish

If a parish cantor is unavailable, guide your group through this section with the information you have gathered.

Prayer Experience

- *Option I:* Gather your group in your prayer center, or in a circle. If possible, prayerfully sing the psalm for the coming Sunday. If this is not possible, have your group recite together one of the psalms from the Living Our Liturgy section.

- *Option II:* Gather your group in your prayer center and sing the song you taught in Lesson 4.

Liturgy of the Word: Second Reading

Objectives

- To understand the nature and role of the second reading.

- To be familiar with the books of the Bible from which the second readings are drawn.

- To grow in their appreciation of the Scriptures as the living word of God.

Preparation

- Read Lesson 7 and its handout in advance.

- In a classroom setting, if you have not already done so, try to arrange to have a parish lector visit your group. The lector can speak about what the ministry means to him or her, and how he or she prepares to proclaim the Scriptures. The lector would be the best person to answer the questions posed in the In Our Parish section.

- If this is not possible, do whatever research is necessary to provide the answers for the In Our Parish section of the lesson.

- In a family setting, if you have not already done so, or if you wish to do so again, plan to introduce yourselves to the lector(s) after Mass this weekend. Thank them for their ministry. Talk with them about how they prepare to proclaim the Scriptures.

- Look up the Scripture citation for the second reading of the coming Sunday.

Supplies

- Sufficient copies of Lesson 7 Handout

- Sufficient pencils or pens

- Sufficient Bibles for your group *or* a resource providing the Scripture of the coming week

Background

The second reading of the liturgy is taken from one of the New Testament books that is *not* a Gospel. Many of these books are letters written by St. Paul or another of the early disciples. It is important to understand that the letters were written to a particular community or person and often address problems or concerns that were prevalent in that community at that time. Understanding these particulars will help us understand the advice we are hearing in the letters. Most Bibles contain introductory material at the beginning of each book that will help you understand the context in which the given book was written. In your own Bible, read the section that pertains to the book from which the coming Sunday's second reading will be taken.

It seems odd to some people that the second reading is not thematically related to the first and second readings for at least half the year—during Ordinary Time. We may think it would be better to choose one that is, or to omit the second reading if it has nothing to do with the others. It is important to realize that the lectionary is not constructed to make the homilist's job easy. Neither is it important that the Scriptures be "boiled down" to a single "theme" for the day. The selection of readings is designed to give the faithful as broad an exposure to Scripture as possible. This was an important goal of the liturgical reform undertaken by the Second Vatican Council. Indeed, the most recently approved lectionary goes still further to provide a wider variety of Scripture proclamations for liturgy. Adults are usually able to hold more than one idea in mind at a time. In Masses with children, provision *is* made for omitting the second reading if that seems appropriate to the age and understanding of the children. In general, however, when it comes to Scripture, less is *not* more.

Introducing the Topic

Explain that today you will be exploring the second reading, and its relation to the Liturgy of the Word. Find out if anyone in your group already knows what books the second reading is taken from. Use their answers as a lead-in to the materials in the handout.

The Scripture

Read aloud the Scripture that begins the lesson. Since this Scripture also began Lesson 4, allow the group to reiterate what they understand of its meaning.

Our Lives

Engage your group in a discussion about how we keep in touch with people who are important to us but not nearby. (They may mention phone calls, e-mail, cards, and letters.)

Read aloud, or have a group member read aloud, the story in the Our Lives section of the handout. Engage the group in a discussion with questions like this:

- **Have you ever been glad to hear from or needed advice from someone you couldn't talk to in person?** *(Allow them to share their experiences.)*

Our Liturgy

Read aloud or silently the Our Liturgy section of the handout. Remind the group of how easy it is for us to contact people we can't see. Mention that in the days of the early church, it would take a long trip to deliver a letter to people who lived some distance from us. Nonetheless, St. Paul and others did write letters, which are now contained in the Christian Scriptures.

Check for content comprehension with questions like these:

- **Who wrote many of the letters included in the Christian Scriptures?** *(St. Paul.)*

- **What were some reasons he wrote these letters?** *(To encourage and advise the Christian churches he had founded and visited.)*

- **When does the second reading correspond with the other two readings?** *(During Advent, the Christmas season, Lent, and the Easter season.)*

- **When does the second reading contain ideas separate from the other two readings?** *(During Ordinary Time.)*

Optional: If time permits, allow the group to look through the New Testament. The letters (also known by their Greek name, *epistles*) offer faith summaries, advice, and answers to a particular community's questions or problems. (Refer to Ephesians 1:3–14 and 1 Corinthians 1:10–17.)

Something to Know

Allow the group time to look over the list of books from which the second reading may be taken. Ask them:

- **How many letters did St. Paul write?** *(13)*

- **How many other letters are there?** *(8)*

- **Which books are not letters?** *(The Acts of Apostles and Revelation.)*

Living Our Liturgy

Have your group read aloud or silently the Living Our Liturgy section of the handout. Be sure they are clear about what it means to refer to Scripture as the inspired word of God. *(Although the words were chosen by the human author, God's Spirit worked through the human author to express God's will and message for us.)*

Something to Do

Provide your group with the citation for the second reading of the coming weekend. Allow the group to prepare their written responses, either individually or in smaller groups.

In Our Parish

The church prefers that there be one lector for the first reading and another for the second. This practice is recommended in order to show the importance of each portion of Scripture that is proclaimed. In many parishes, a variety of factors may make this difficult or impossible. If no lector is available to answer this question, learn what choice your parish has made and why.

Prayer Experience

Gather your group in a prayer center, or in a circle. Sing the song you taught in Lesson 4. Then proclaim Ephesians 1:15–19. Conclude by blessing your group with this blessing from Numbers 6:24–26. Extend your right hand over the group as you say:

The Lord bless you and keep you;
The Lord make his face to shine upon you and be gracious to you;
The Lord lift up his countenance upon you and give you peace.

Liturgy of the Word: Gospel

Objectives

- To understand the role of the Gospel reading at liturgy.

- To know the responses and postures appropriate to the proclamation of the Gospel.

- To appreciate the Gospels as the Good News of Jesus Christ for our salvation.

Preparation

- Read Lesson 8 and its handout in advance.

- Do the research that will allow you to provide the answers to the In Our Parish section.

- *Optional:* Be prepared to sing, or play an audiotape of, one or more settings of the "Alleluia" used as the Gospel acclamation in your parish. During Lent, learn the alternate Gospel acclamation.

Supplies

- Sufficient copies of Lesson 8 Handout

- Sufficient pens or pencils

- Sufficient Bibles for your group, or another resource containing the Sunday Scriptures

- *Optional:* tape player and cassette of "Alleluia" settings

Background

The Gospel of Jesus Christ is the heart of our Christian faith. It stands to reason then, that the proclamation of the Gospel reading at liturgy is the high point of the Liturgy of the Word. The Bible contains four accounts of Jesus' ministry, passion, death, and resurrection. Most Bibles contain introductory material at the beginning of each of the Gospels. Look there to learn more about the similarities, differences, and defining characteristics of each of the four accounts.

Each week at liturgy, another episode from the life of Jesus is recounted in the Gospel. It is important to understand that this recounting is not meant to be chronological or biographical. Instead, it is a recounting of the story of faith and salvation. The Good News of Jesus is so rich, so multifaceted, so beyond our imagining, that we gather week after week to hear the entire story unfold.

Lectionary Cycles

Among the reforms of the liturgy undertaken as a result of the Second Vatican Council was the revision of the lectionary. Prior to the Council, the Scriptures were proclaimed in a one-year cycle, with the readings repeating on the same Sunday each year. The church wanted the wealth of the Scriptures to be more available to the faithful, so a three-year cycle of readings was devised. The most recent edition of the American lectionary includes even more Scripture by offering three-year cycles for certain feasts that had previously had just one set of readings.

The lectionary cycles are named simply with the first three letters of the alphabet. Year A is the year of Matthew's Gospel. Year B is the year of Mark's Gospel, and Year C is the year of Luke's Gospel. The Gospel of John is proclaimed in each of these cycles during the Easter season. Because Mark's Gospel is shorter than the other two, portions of the Gospel of John are also added to Cycle B during Ordinary Time. The lectionary, then, provides us with a much larger portion of the Bible than ever before.

The lectionary approach to Scripture asks us to consider how these two or three readings, plus the psalm, speak God's word to us together. It is also important to remember that each of these readings is taken from a larger work, with its own context and purpose. An appreciation of the Scripture passage in its original context and purpose will enhance our ability to appreciate how the readings for a given week speak to us as a set. When you prepare the Scriptures at home in preparation for liturgy, it may be helpful to refer back to the original chapter and book from which the passage is taken. For liturgical purposes, we look at how the readings and psalm each impinge on, enhance, relate to, or expound on what the other is saying.

Introducing Topic

Explain that today you will be exploring the third and most important of the Scripture readings at Mass—the Gospel. Ask what your group already knows about the Gospels and use that as the springboard into this lesson.

The Scripture

Read aloud the Scripture quotation that begins the lesson. Allow the group to express their understanding of what it means. (Knowing and living the Gospel is a way of life that continues past physical death.)

Our Lives

Read aloud, or have a group member read aloud the Our Lives section of the handout. Ask the group if they can recall a time when they had good news to tell. Allow them to share their stories of what it felt like to tell good news. Be prepared with your own story as well.

Our Liturgy

Explain to your group that the word "Gospel" means "good news." Ask them why the story of Jesus is called Good News. (Because Jesus shows us how much God loves us. Because Jesus shows us that everyone is equal in God's eyes, which is certainly "Good News" for the lowly, poor, and outcasts. Because Jesus shows us how to have eternal life. Because Jesus shows us how to be happy doing God's will. Because Jesus shows us a better way.)

Have the group read the section aloud or silently. Ask the group to recount their recollections of Gospel stories with questions like these:

- **Can anyone recall a Gospel story that tells us about Jesus' teaching?**

- **Can any one recall a Gospel story about a miracle Jesus did?**

- **Can anyone recall a Gospel story about how people reacted to Jesus?**

Something to Know

Give your group time to review silently the descriptions in the Something to Know section. Be sure the group understands how the lectionary cycles are set up. Be sure everyone knows what lectionary cycle is currently being used and what Gospel is being proclaimed.

Have the group practice aloud the dialogue that precedes and closes the proclamation of the Gospel. One person says the priest's part, prompting all to say the response. Continue until they respond with confidence.

Living Our Liturgy

After reading this section, have your group offer specific examples of those who need to hear the Good News of Jesus.

Something to Do

Allow your group time to read and respond to the Gospel for the coming Sunday. If your group is large, allow the members to work in pairs or triads. If time allows, lead them in sharing their responses with the entire group.

The Scripture

Reread the Scripture passage for this lesson. Ask the group if they have any additional insights into the meaning of this quotation and how it relates to today's topic. Summarize their original responses, and any others they now have. Lead them to understand that the Good News of Jesus is this: The kind of life Jesus asks us to live is the kind of life that continues even after we die. It starts now and keeps on going.

In Our Parish

Use your voice or an audiotape to familiarize or review with the group one or more settings of the "Alleluia" used in your parish as Gospel acclamations. During Lent, sing the alternate Gospel acclamation. Describe, or have a group member describe, the movement that takes place during the singing of the Gospel acclamation.

Prayer Experience

- *Option I:* Gather your group in a prayer center, or in a circle. Sing a Gospel acclamation. Proclaim the Gospel for the coming Sunday, and sing the Gospel acclamation again.

- *Option II:* Gather your group in a prayer center or in a circle. Sing the song you taught in Lesson 4.

Liturgy of the Word: Homily, Creed, and Prayer of the Faithful

Objectives

- To appreciate the role of the homily, Creed, and prayer of the faithful in the Liturgy of the Word.

- To appreciate the significance and responsibility of the homilist.

- To understand the nature of the Creed and prayer of the faithful.

Preparation

- Read Lesson 9 and its handout in advance.

- Do the research that will allow you to provide the answers to the In Our Parish section. In speaking with the person who prepares the prayer of the faithful, ask what process is used to determine the intercessions for each week.

- *Optional:* If possible, arrange for someone who preaches in your parish to speak with your group, or speak with him after Mass. Ask about how he prepares the homily, and what it means to him to preach about God's word.

- *Optional:* If possible, arrange for someone who prepares the prayer of the faithful to speak with your group. Have him or her address the question of how the petitions and the response are determined.

Supplies

- Sufficient copies of Lesson 9 Handout

- Sufficient Bibles, or other resource containing the Sunday Scriptures

- Sufficient copies of your parish worship aid, or other resource containing the Creed your parish uses

- Sufficient pens or pencils

- Writing paper

- *Optional:* sufficient copies of the After-Mass Worksheet

Background

The restoration of scriptural preaching is another gift of the Second Vatican Council. The "sermons" of the pre-Council days, sometimes well prepared and thought provoking, sometimes read from a "script" provided by the bishop, were nonetheless instructions of a more catechetical nature. There was no expectation that the sermon be related to the Scriptures of the day. There was no expectation that preaching take place at daily Masses. Now, at every liturgy, we have come to treasure the homily as our opportunity to gain additional insight into the Scriptures proclaimed that day. This is evidenced by the fact that the homily is the part of the Mass most likely to draw both compliments and criticism for the presider. The responsibility to know the Scriptures well and to be truly in touch with the assembly is one of the most important responsibilities of those who preach. They deserve our congratulations when they succeed and our guidance when they falter.

Both the Apostles' Creed and the Nicene Creed are ancient faith formularies dating back to the earliest years of the church (the year 325 for the Nicene Creed, earlier for the Apostles' Creed). Though not the only creeds the church has ever produced, these two have achieved a certain "pride of place" among the creeds, being deemed both the most ancient and the most faithful to the faith of the apostles and their first followers.

The prayer of the faithful is exactly what it says: the prayer of all the baptized. That is why catechumens and the elect are dismissed before the prayer of the faithful begins. They do not yet share in the *priestly* role of the People of God to intercede on behalf of others.

It is important to understand that the prayer of the faithful are *intercessory* prayers. They are not, for instance, prayers of thanksgiving. So we would not pray, "In thanksgiving for the recent rain that has ended our drought," but rather, "That God will continue to send the rains that have ended our drought."

Like the intercessions themselves, responses to the prayer of the faithful are chosen by the individual parish. They can vary widely, but seem best when kept short and easy to remember. It is a wonderful feature of the collective Catholic consciousness that, unless instructed otherwise, people will always respond "Lord, hear our prayer." Intercessory prayer has thus become part and parcel of our Catholic being.

Introducing the Topic

Briefly find out what your group already knows about the homily, the Creed, and the prayer of the faithful. Use the Something to Know section to make it clear which parts of the liturgy are under discussion. This will allow everyone to use the correct terms with understanding, and make discussion easier.

The Scripture

Read aloud the Scripture that opens this lesson. Allow your group to share their ideas about its meaning. (This describes how the earliest Christians spent their time; listening to their leaders was important to them; being together to pray was important to them.)

Our Lives

Have your group read the story of the Scout troop aloud or silently. Provide a lead-in to the next section with questions like these:

- **Why did the less-experienced Scouts need guides?** *(They had never done this before; without guides, they might not know which way to go or how to handle certain situations.)*

- **What made the older Scouts good guides?** *(They had done this before; they had checked out the trail in advance; they knew the way and what to look out for.)*

- **How were the older Scouts able to help the younger ones?** *(They could show them things the younger ones didn't know; they could teach them the way; they could show them how to live outdoors.)*

- **At Mass, who guides us as we try to understand the Scriptures?** *(Those who preach.)*

Our Liturgy

If you have not already done so, review the terms in the Something to Know section before reading further.

Have your group read the beginning of this section (about the homily and the Creed) aloud or silently. Check for comprehension with questions like these:

- **How is the homilist like a guide on a journey?** *(He shows people the way to God by explaining the Scriptures.)*

- **What makes the homilist a good guide?** *(He is usually more experienced with the Scriptures so he should be a good guide; he can help people see things in the Scriptures that they might not have seen without him; he checks out the Scriptures in advance and prepares how he will guide people; he studies and prays with the Scriptures throughout his life.)*

To explore the Creed, ask your group about other statements of belief with which they may be familiar (Scout pledge; a class "mission statement"; the Declaration of Independence.)

If your group knows it, have them recite the Creed used at weekend liturgies in your parish. If they do not know it, read it to them. And then ask them:

- **Why do you think we recite the Creed near the end of the Liturgy of the Word?** *(After we've heard the Scriptures and had them explained to us, we declare our faith in Jesus' teachings. We make our faith statement before we move on to the Liturgy of the Eucharist.)*

Have your group read the remainder of the Our Liturgy section (about the prayer of the faithful). Ask them to give examples of petitions they have heard prayed in their parish. Then conduct a review for comprehension:

- **What kind of prayers are these?** *(Prayers of petition; "asking" prayers.)*

- **What are some other names for the prayer of the faithful?** *(universal prayer; general intercessions)*

- **For whom do we pray in the prayer of the faithful?** *(The church; the world; people in need; ourselves; the sick; the deceased.)*

If the person responsible for composing the prayer of the faithful is available to speak to your group, have him or her do so now. This might be the best person to guide your group through the Something to Do activity.

Living Our Liturgy

Have your group read this section aloud or silently. Explore the idea of "journey" with questions like these:

- **Why do we say that we are on a journey with God?** *(Getting to know God can take a long time; when we grow in faith and in our relationship with God, it's like traveling along a road from one place to another; depending on where we are on our journey, we will have different experiences of God and people, just as we have different experiences when we are traveling.)*

- **Who is with us on this journey?** *(God; the people of God in our parish; the priests who guide us; other leaders or companions particular to our parish.)*

- **How does the Liturgy of the Word help us in our journey with God?** *(Accept all reasonable responses.)*

Something to Do

Guide your group through this activity, using the Bibles, paper, and pens you have provided.

In Our Parish

If you are not able to speak with a homilist or the person who prepares the intercessions, guide your group through this section with the information you gathered in advance.

Prayer Experience

- *Option I:* Gather your group in a prayer center, or in a circle. Determine an appropriate response. *(Lord, hear our prayer; Hear us, O Lord; We love you, Lord, let us grow in trust.)* Then pray the petitions written by your group in response to the Something to Do activity. Allow the group to add petitions spontaneously as well.

- *Option II:* Gather your group in a prayer center or in a circle. Sing the song you taught in Lesson 4.

Liturgy of the Eucharist: Overview of Meal and Sacrifice

Objectives

- To appreciate the liturgy as a meal.

- To appreciate the liturgy as the sacrifice of Jesus.

- To connect our daily experience of meal and sacrifice to the liturgical experience of meal and sacrifice.

Preparation

- Read Lesson 10 and its handout in advance.

- As background for explaining why Jesus is called the "Lamb of God," be sure you are familiar with the story of the first Passover and the freeing of the Israelites from Egypt. You will find the most pertinent material in the Book of Exodus, Chapters 11 and 12.

- Be prepared to answer the questions in the In Our Parish section. Using your voice, a tape, or a prepared student leader, be able to lead your group in singing a "Lamb of God" litany used in your parish. If necessary, consult the music director or other parish personnel to determine which musical setting is currently in use.

Supplies

- Sufficient copies of Lesson 10 Handout

- Sufficient pens or pencils

- *Optional:* drawing materials

- *Optional:* sufficient copies of the After-Mass Worksheet

Background

The recovery of the Catholic understanding of the liturgy as a meal has been one of the great gifts of the Second Vatican Council. When we think of ourselves as a family gathered for a meal, we open up important implications for our relationship with Jesus and our relationship with one another. We realize, for instance, that it is Jesus who is the host at this banquet, not the priest or other ministers. We realize, too, that the practice of hospitality is as important at church, if not more so, as when people gather in our homes for a meal. We realize our oneness at the table of the Lord.

Some may see the emphasis on Eucharist as a meal as detracting from the sacredness of the liturgical action. On the contrary, meal theology is a logical outgrowth of incarnational theology. As he did many times during his earthly life, Jesus calls his followers together to eat with him. Jesus chose to be remembered through this everyday human activity. This is just another way in which God shares our human nature. Through the very natural events of human existence, we are made holy.

The sacrificial nature of the liturgy has long been a focal point of eucharistic theology. Pre–Vatican II Catholics surely remember being taught that the Mass is the un-bloody re-presentation of the sacrifice of Calvary. To really appreciate what this means, it helps to know more about sacrifices in Old Testament days.

In ancient times, the slaughter of an animal was the sign of a covenant made between two kings. The animal would be split in two, and the kings would walk between the two halves of the animal. This meant: "May what has happened to this animal happen to me if I break this covenant with you."

We see something similar, though un-bloody, in the breaking of the bread. The large host is broken in two and the precious Blood is poured into cups. Jesus, the Lamb of God, is the sacrifice of the New Covenant. Through his crucified body and his blood spilled on Calvary, God entered into a New Covenant with us. Through his Body broken in the consecrated bread and his Blood poured into cups for us to drink, the covenant is renewed. The sacrifice of Calvary is present again.

Because of the proximity of Jesus' death to Passover, the imagery of the paschal lamb clearly spoke to the early Christians of their salvation in Christ. Thus, the lamb sacrificed for the salvation of the Israelites during the Exodus, and the foundation of the first covenant, became the Lamb of God, whose blood saves us all from slavery to sin and puts us in a new covenant relationship with God. It is not a covenant of law, as was the first, but a covenant of faith in Christ Jesus.

You can see, then, how important the actions of the breaking and pouring really are. This is not simply a practical moment, accompanied by lots of hubbub at the altar and the scurrying of ministers as hosts are placed in multiple ciboria and the eucharistic wine is poured into multiple chalices. No, this breaking and pouring is the action of Jesus sacrificing himself for our freedom. This is the action of God entering into a covenant with us. The action should not be obscured but seen and savored. The accompanying litany need not be threefold but should take as long as the action itself takes.

By participating in the Eucharist, we are accepting our part in this covenant. We mean "May I be broken like this bread for the sake of the Gospel. May my life be poured out for the sake of my brothers and sisters in faith. May the sacrifice of Jesus become my sacrifice as I strive to live the Christian way."

Both meal theology and sacrifice theology help us to see the centrality of sharing Christ's Body and Blood when celebrating Mass. Would you respond to an invitation to share a meal and *not* eat? Would you witness

God entering into a covenant with you and *not* accept your part in it? The purpose of the liturgy is to draw us to that table, to draw us into that covenant. Everyone who possibly can be, *should* be in the communion procession.

Introducing the Topic

Explain to your group that you are going to explore two important ways of understanding the liturgy, especially the Liturgy of the Eucharist. Then ask the following questions:

- **Why do you think we say the liturgy is a meal?** *(Because we eat and drink; because we remember what Jesus did at the Last Supper; because we all sit around a big table.)*

- **Why do you think we say that the liturgy is the sacrifice of Jesus?** *(This may be more difficult for the group to answer; accept all reasonable responses for now.)*

Suggest that they stay alert for more ways to understand both of these concepts of liturgy.

The Scripture

Have someone in the group read aloud the Scripture quotation. Do not ask for input on this now, but suggest that they will be able to comment on this Scripture better at the end of the lesson. Remember to come back to it before concluding.

Our Lives

Have the group read the Our Lives section aloud or silently. Help them explore the meaning of the story with questions like these:

- **Why do you think Elizabeth's family was having a party for her grandparents?** *(Because it was such a special occasion; everyone wanted to be together for the celebration.)*

- **Why do you think that celebrating and eating always go together?** *(Eating together unites us. Offering food to guests is the way we show them they are welcome in our home; People who share an important experience, such as the birth of a baby or a wedding, or a birthday, always eat together. Even a sorrowful event, like a funeral, is usually followed by a meal. It's the way people express their togetherness.)*

- **Why do you think Elizabeth's grandma said her renewal of vows "felt pretty real"? Why did she feel as though it was her "wedding day all over again" and that the vows meant more now than they did the first time?** *(After being married for fifty years, she had experienced what it meant to be married. She had lived her vows "for better or for worse, in sickness and in health." All the emotions and experiences of marriage were happening when they said the vows the second time. So it felt like getting married again.)*

Our Liturgy

Have your group read the Living Our Liturgy/The Mass Is a Meal section aloud or silently. Check for comprehension with questions like these:

- **Give some examples of times when sharing food helps people get closer.** *(Any special family occasion, like Christmas, Thanksgiving, a wedding. Children should be able to talk about how sitting together at lunch helps their friendships grow stronger. Grown-ups who want to get to know one another better often go out to eat.)*

- **Why do you think Jesus chose a meal as the way in which he wants us to remember him?** *(Because it's a normal human event; it's a human sign of unity; it's something that happens every day so it's easy for us to understand.)*

- **In what ways does the Mass look like a meal?** *(There's a table and food; we get to eat and drink.)*

Something to Do

Allow your group time to complete this exercise, then review their responses

At a Special Meal:	At a Mass:
We invite people to join us.	*People gather at church; Jesus calls us to join him; We are always responding to Jesus' invitation when we come to Mass.*
We greet our guests.	*We welcome others before Mass; we exchange the sign of peace.*
We share our stories.	*The Scriptures are read.*
We set the table.	*The altar is prepared.*
We get the food ready.	*The bread and wine is brought to the table.*
We eat and drink.	*We come to communion; we eat and drink the Body and Blood of Christ.*
We clear the table.	*The altar is cleared.*

The Mass Is a Sacrifice

Have your group read this section aloud or silently. Check for comprehension with questions like these:

- **What were some of the sacrifices Jesus made during his lifetime?** *(Summarize from the first paragraph.)*

- **Why do we call Jesus the "Lamb of God"?** (*Jesus is like the Passover lamb because his blood saves us from our sins just like the blood of the first Passover lamb saved the Israelites from slavery in Egypt. The slaughter of the Passover lamb was the sign of the first covenant; Jesus' death is the sign of the new covenant.*)

- **Why do we say that the Mass is a sacrifice?** (*What happened at Calvary is happening again, only now it is happening with bread and wine that have become the Body and Blood of Jesus instead of with Jesus' original human body.*)

Optional Activity: Have your group make drawings that depict "meal" and "sacrifice." Suggest that they display these with their drawings of "listening" and "responding" from Lesson 4. Together, these will provide a visual summary of the liturgy. Allow them to share and describe their drawing with the group.

Living Our Liturgy

Have your group read this section aloud or silently. See if your group can provide examples of each type of sacrifice. (Instances of peer pressure will provide examples in the first two cases. You may be able to speak about the work of missionaries. If the group is unfamiliar with people losing their lives in service of the Gospel, speak to them about Archbishop Oscar Romero of El Salvador, the murdered missionaries in El Salvador, or other situations with which you may be familiar. Other examples of sacrifice can be drawn from the lives of those who risk or accept arrest to protest racial injustice or weapons development and proliferation.)

Something to Do

Allow your group to complete and share their responses to this section.

In Our Parish

- Discuss with your group what you see when the Eucharist is being prepared for distribution.

- Lead your group in singing a "Lamb of God" litany from your assembly's repertoire.

Prayer Experience

Gather your group in a prayer center or in a circle.

Leader: Gracious God,

Your call draws us to your table and into
your covenant.

When we share food with others, when we
make loving sacrifices,

Your Spirit lives in us. Grant that we who eat
and drink with you

will have the courage to make the sacrifices
that bring life to others.

We ask this through Christ our Lord.

Liturgy of the Eucharist: Giving Thanks

Objectives

- To recognize thanksgiving as key to the eucharistic action.

- To understand how the Liturgy of the Eucharist expresses thanksgiving.

- To be familiar with the elements of the Liturgy of the Eucharist.

- To connect our everyday experience of gratitude with our liturgical expression of gratitude.

Preparation

- Read Lesson 11 and its handout in advance.

- Something to Know: Be sure you can give at least a brief description of what we see and do at each of the parts of the eucharistic prayer.

- If possible, invite a priest to meet with your group to show them the sacramentary. He might also be the best candidate to offer the descriptions required in the Something to Know section.

Supplies

- Sufficient copies of Lesson 11 Handout

- Sufficient pens or pencils

- *Optional:* sufficient copies of the After-Mass Worksheet

Background

In exploring the meaning of gratitude, this chapter attempts to get beyond the "say thank you" approach we use with the youngest children. We try to take them further by helping them discover moments of gratitude in their lives. This spontaneous welling-up of gratitude is a spiritual capacity that needs to be at the heart of our relationships with one another and with God. By helping people look for the *surprising* ways in which we are cared for, we can begin to see that *all* of the ways God cares for us are causes for gratitude, since we can never claim that God *owes* us anything.

Thanksgiving is at the heart of the Eucharist, and indeed is the meaning of the word. That God should become a person, live with us, die, and be raised again for our salvation may be the greatest surprise of all. This and all our individual experiences of God's providence come together to form the nucleus of our praise in the eucharistic prayer.

Introducing the Topic

Begin by asking the group to describe a time when they were grateful. Lead into the lesson by advising them that being grateful is at the heart of our eucharistic celebration.

The Scripture

Have a member of the group read the Scripture aloud. Ask them what "victory" we have to be grateful for. (Responses should focus on: We can be victorious over sin because we participate in the life of Jesus. We have been given the same victory as Jesus—the victory of eternal life.)

Our Lives

Read the story aloud or silently. Help the group connect with the meaning of the story with questions like these:

- **What surprised Manuel?** (*Manuel was surprised that Mr. Rosario noticed his confusion. He was also surprised that Mr. Rosario would spend extra time with him to help him.*)

- **Why might Manuel have been surprised by that?** (*Manuel might have felt that he was just a regular kid, no one special, just a member of the class. He was surprised that the teacher would pay attention to his individual needs.*)

Allow the group to continue reading the last paragraph of this section. Ask them what the difference is between saying "thank you" and being grateful. (Saying "thank you" can sometimes just be a way to show good manners; gratitude comes from the heart. It often comes from the experience of being cared for when we didn't expect it, or maybe when we didn't think we deserved it.)

Our Liturgy

Ask your group to name some of the ways we can tell that God is looking out for us. (*Accept all reasonable answers.*) Then have them read this section aloud or silently. Check for comprehension with questions like these:

- **What are some ways we express gratitude in the Liturgy of the Eucharist?** (*By making a sacrificial offering in the collection; in the offering prayers over the bread and wine; in the preface before we sing the "Holy."*)

- **What do you think is the most important thing we have to be grateful for?** (*God's gift of Jesus.*)

Something to Know

Review the information in this section. An enjoyable way to review the parts of the Liturgy of the Eucharist would be to have members of the group demonstrate what happens at each part. Let different members show the role of the presider, the cantor, the servers, the assembly, and so forth.

Living Our Liturgy
Something to Do

Allow your group to review the activity. Give them time to complete the portion that corresponds to the day on which you are meeting. Suggest that they meditate on what they've written just before attending Mass this weekend. Perhaps this will make it easier for them to celebrate with gratitude.

In Our Parish

If a priest is available to meet with your group, he could show them the sacramentary. If not, it may be possible to speak with him after Mass this weekend.

Prayer Experience

Gather your group in a prayer center, or in a circle. Allow time for a prayerful silence to develop. Create a litany of thanksgiving by allowing members of the group to mention things for which they are grateful. Instruct them to respond with: *We thank you, Lord.* Follow this pattern:

Individual: For _____,

All: *We thank you Lord.*

Conclude with a prayer of your own, or one like this:

Loving God, all that we have and all that we are is from you.
Help us to grow closer to you by seeing your wondrous love
   in everything around us.
We make this prayer in the name of Jesus, the Lord. Amen.

Liturgy of the Eucharist: Remembering and Ritual

Objectives

- To understand and appreciate the role of ritual in our lives.

- To appreciate the ritual nature of the liturgy.

- To appreciate that while elements of ritual can change, the heart of the ritual does not.

Preparation

- Read Lesson 12 and its handout in advance.

- If possible, arrange to speak with a priest after Mass or arrange for a priest to visit your group to demonstrate and discuss the gestures used at liturgy.

- Learn to sing, enlist the aid of a singer, or secure an audiotape of "Song of the Body of Christ" by David Haas (GIA Publications Inc., 1989).

- If you do not remember liturgy before the Second Vatican Council, enlist the aid of someone who does to help your group understand how liturgy can change.

- If your time is limited, consider dividing this lesson into two or three shorter sessions. In the first, explore the Our Lives section. In the second, complete the lesson, or save the Something to Know section for a third session.

Supplies

- Sufficient copies of Lesson 12 Handout

- Sufficient pencils or pens

- *Optional:* magazine pictures of a variety of people that seem to show emotion or temperament

- *Optional:* audio equipment to play "Song of the Body of Christ"

Background

At the heart of this lesson is the role of liturgy *as ritual*. Families and cultures have many rituals on which their self-definition depends. It is important here to understand that we are not referring to private or individual rituals, like bringing a pink elephant figurine to a bingo game. Rather, we are referring to rituals that belong to a group, in this case, the church.

It is completely proper to the nature of human beings to express themselves in outward ways and to express their most important beliefs in ritual. Ritual joins us with others who believe as we do. Ritual expresses the inner feelings and beliefs of believers. Ritual expresses and defines who we are.

The story of Allison's birthday is the "hook" on which we will "hang" our understanding of ritual. Children can easily understand why Allison *needed* a birthday party to make it feel as though it was her birthday. But there are subtler points to draw out as well. Through the story, help the children understand that some elements of our ritual can change, but that the essence of the ritual cannot. For example, Allison did not bring cupcakes to school for her birthday as she had done in the past. She had outgrown that part of the ritual and it no longer had the meaning it once had. But Allison *was* old enough now to cut and serve the cake herself. It would have been foolish for her to refuse to do this simply because she had not done it on any prior birthdays. In fact, that would have been a denial of the very growth the birthday celebrates! As Allison grew and changed, appropriate adjustments in the way she participated in the birthday rituals were made.

But the heart of the ritual did not change. There was still a birthday cake, candles, the singing of "Happy Birthday," gifts, and guests. It should be easy for the children to see why the suggested birthday "celebration" in the Something to Do section wouldn't work. That's just not how we do it! Such a made-up ritual does not have the power of group ownership behind it.

This parallels the church's understanding of Mass. Some elements of the ritual change as our understanding grows and changes. The church eliminates parts of the ritual that no longer speak to us and adjusts how we do others. Nonetheless, the heart of the ritual remains the same. Just as it would be foolish to cling to pieces of a ritual that no longer express our self-understanding or even deny it, it would be meaningless to change substantial portions of the liturgy simply for the sake of change. In fact ritual *only* has meaning when it remains substantially the same. It is the repetition of the ritual that gives it meaning, and that allows the group to own it. Just as salad instead of birthday cake is meaningless, so change for its own sake has no place in liturgy. In this way, you can help the children see that, while there is room for appropriate changes, the repetitive nature of the liturgy is a positive element, not a negative one. This should help those children who are bored at Mass because "it's the same thing every week." Their boredom may be real, but the antidote is in helping them to understand, own, and enter into the ritual, not in changing it simply for the sake of increased entertainment value. You are helping them do exactly that through the use of *Learning about Liturgy*.

In reviewing the meaning of gestures, it is important not to assign one single meaning to the gestures used at Mass. By their very nature, symbolic actions have many layers of meaning. One individual may see something another has not seen. It would be better to ask, "How does this gesture look to you?" or "How does it feel when you see (or do) this gesture?" Then accept all reasonable answers. Avoid giving the impression that gestures can be assigned a single meaning as if they were mathematical equations. The same would be true for any other symbol or symbolic action.

Introducing the Topic

Refer to the Something to Know section if they are unfamiliar with the meaning of the word "ritual." Ask your group to mention some rituals with which they are familiar.

The Scripture

Have someone read aloud the Scripture from the first letter to the Corinthians. Then ask:

- **Did you ever realize that you were proclaiming the Lord's death by participating in the Eucharist?**

- **What can you point to in the liturgy that indicates we are proclaiming the Lord's death?** *(The priest always tells about Jesus' death in the eucharistic prayer; we are doing the same thing Jesus did right before he died.)*

Our Lives

Summarize in your own words, or have someone read aloud, the section entitled Seeing What's on the Inside. Give examples, and ask the children for examples, of how people show their feelings and even their personalities in their faces and body language. Emotions like joy, fear, sorrow, and anger are often easy to distinguish. You may also be able to help the group describe subtler emotions like boredom, frustration, or nervousness. Ask the group to show you a facial expression that might accompany each of these feelings, or to show you how *they* look when they are feeling these emotions.

- **Can you tell what kind of a mood your friend is in as soon as you see him or her? How?**

- **Can you tell what kind of a day Mom or Dad had as soon as she or he gets in from work? How?**

- **Do you think that the way a person walks can give a hint as to what kind of person he or she is?** *(Help the group identify body language that indicates whether a person is generally content or overburdened, such as a lively step or stooped shoulders.)*

- **What are some other outward ways people have of letting you know who they are and what they are into?** *(This may include a discussion of clothing styles, tattoos, jewelry, and the like.)*

Optional: Use the pictures you have prepared to talk about how people express their inner feelings and nature in their outer appearance. Show each picture and ask what the individual may be feeling. Ask the group if they have any clues as to what type of individual this might be. (Accept all reasonable answers.)

Our Lives — Ritual

Read aloud, or have a group member read aloud, the story of Allison's birthday. At the end of the first paragraph, ask if anyone in the group has ever had a similar experience. Allow a few moments for responses.

Continue reading the story. Ask the group why they think Saturday felt more like Allison's birthday than Thursday. (Because she didn't do any "birthday things" on Thursday; because the cake and the party are what "make" a birthday. Help the children understand that simply knowing it was her birthday wasn't enough. Celebrating the standard birthday rituals made it real.)

Our Liturgy

Have the group read the first paragraph in this section silently or aloud.

Activity: If your group is large enough, have the members work in smaller groups of two or three. If your group is small enough, have the whole group work together. List their responses to this question: When you look at the Mass, can you tell what God's people believe? What does the Mass tell us about our faith and beliefs? (Try to get them to look at the Mass itself, not the content of the Scriptures or homily.) (Possible responses: We believe that Jesus died on the cross for us; that's why we carry the cross in the procession. We believe that Jesus is speaking to us in the Scriptures; we can tell from how we pay attention and make a procession with the Gospel. We believe that this is really special because everything we use is fancy—like the priest's clothes and the chalice. We believe that the bread and wine become the Body and Blood of Jesus; we can tell from the words the priest says in the eucharistic prayer and from how he holds it up for us to look at.)

Continue reading the second paragraph. Explain that Mass does for Catholics what the birthday party did for Allison's family. Allison is important to them, so they got together to express that. Jesus is important to us so we get together to express that. Allison needed to be with the people who loved her. We need to be with the people who love Jesus.

Ritual helps us experience what's important to us. Allison didn't feel as though it was her birthday until she participated in the birthday ritual with her family. We can't feel what Jesus' death and resurrection means unless we participate in the liturgy. Ritual helps turn knowledge into experience.

Have your group complete the second question in the Something to Do section. Then, ask your group:

- **Which elements of the birthday ritual *had* changed as Allison got older?** *(She no longer brought cupcakes for her class; she could cut and serve the cake herself.)*

- **Why did these elements change?** *(Allison grew up. She wasn't little anymore and could do things differently. The changes were a better expression of who Allison had become.)*

Have the group share their answers to the Something to Do question. Help them focus on the idea that this would be *too much* change, and no one would understand the new ritual. This new ritual is not a shared and commonly held way of celebrating birthdays, but the pointless invention of an individual. Everything that makes a birthday a birthday would be missing!

Now relate these changes to the liturgy by asking questions like "Have you ever seen anything change in the way we do Mass?" (Responses may focus on seasonal changes, or on procedural changes particular to your parish.)

Describe or have an older adult describe some of the changes in the liturgy brought about by the Second Vatican Council. (The language of the Mass became the vernacular instead of Latin; the priest faced the people instead of having his back to them; the assembly was given an active role instead of just watching the priest.)

Ask the group why they think the church made these changes and adjustments. (So we could pray the liturgy better, and better understand what we were praying; so the priest's role as a member of the assembly would be more apparent; so the liturgy could belong to all God's people and not just to the priest.) (Be prepared to discuss the reasons for any local adjustments as well. For instance, how singing the penitential rite during Lent helps us focus on the meaning of the season.)

Lead the group to conclude that the church is wise to make changes in the way we celebrate when these changes are meant to better reflect our understanding of Jesus and to help us experience God's action in our lives more fully.

Finally, ask the group what *does not* change at the liturgy. (The liturgy is always a gathering of God's people; we always listen to the Scripture; the liturgy is always a memorial of Jesus' death and resurrection.)

Introduce "Song of the Body of Christ" by David Haas. Indicate to the group that this song, especially the refrain, is a good summary of what is essential in liturgy. Help them learn to sing it.

Something to Know

Review the two definitions given. Have the group complete the first question in the Something to Do section, and share their answers.

Ask the children to give examples of familiar gestures or demonstrate gestures and to supply the meaning. (Possible responses: Your index finger pointed at me means I'm in trouble or being scolded. A handshake means I'm welcoming you or glad to meet you. A hug means we're close, or I'm taking care of you or comforting the one I'm hugging. An index finger placed over the lips is a sign to be quiet. An index finger bending quickly up and down is a sign to "come here." An index finger pointed at my head and rotating means I'm a little crazy.)

If a priest is available to visit your group, have him demonstrate some gestures used at Mass. Or, ask the group to give examples of some gestures used at Mass, or demonstrate them yourself. Ask questions like these:

- **What does this gesture seem to mean? What does this gesture feel like to you?** *(Allow all reasonable answers.)*

- **What would the liturgy be like if there were no gestures, just words?** *(Responses will probably indicate that this would be boring; that it wouldn't mean anything.)*

Guide your group to see that the gestures of the ritual help give expression to the words, so that we are more involved in the prayer and can express our faith better.

In Our Parish

- Allow time for your group to complete this section and share their responses.

- Or, ask your group to complete the final section after attending Mass this weekend.

Be sure to begin your next session with a review of their responses.

Prayer Experience

Gather your group in a prayer center, or in a circle. To focus your prayer around a ritual action, have your group hold hands and pray any prayer they know by heart. Then have the members of the group bless one another by tracing the sign of the cross on one another's foreheads. Conclude with a sign of peace.

Liturgy of the Eucharist: Remembering and Making Present

Objectives

- To appreciate the gift and the power of memory.
- To understand the liturgy as the memorial of Christ's sacrifice on the cross.
- To appreciate the way in which memory and ritual, through the power of the Holy Spirit, *make present* the paschal mystery.

Preparation

- Read Lesson 13 and its handout in advance.
- For the In Our Parish section be able to sing, or engage the assistance of someone who can sing, the memorial acclamation(s) used in your parish.
- *Prayer Option I:* prepare to lead your group in singing "Song of the Body of Christ" by David Haas (GIA Publications, Inc., 1989), or "We Remember" by Marty Haugen (GIA Publications, Inc., 1980)

Supplies

- Sufficient copies of Lesson 13 Handout
- Sufficient pens or pencils
- *Optional:* drawing paper and a coloring medium
- *Optional:* sufficient copies of the After-Mass Worksheet

Background

Lesson 13 draws us further into the heart of the Liturgy of the Eucharist. Just as the Liturgy of the Word drew us into some aspect of the paschal mystery, so now the eucharistic prayer draws us further into the heart of the paschal mystery—the death and resurrection of Jesus. The pattern of Jesus' sacrificial love is the style of living we are called to take on as our own. Through the liturgy, the memorial of Christ's sacrifice, we are formed more and more into the image of Christ.

This lesson hangs on the difference between mere recall and the kind of remembering that *makes present*. Perhaps you have had the experience of owning a special object or keepsake that had belonged to a loved one. The value of that object is not really in the object itself, but in the way in which that object allows the person to be present to you through it. All that the person means to you is brought back through that one object.

This is how it is with the Eucharist. All that Jesus means to us is brought back and *truly present* when we remember through ritual his Passover from death to life. By joining ourselves with one another and the Holy Spirit, this remembering allows us to conform our lives more and more to the pattern of Jesus' life, the pattern of self-sacrificing love and undaunted faithfulness to God's ways.

Introducing the Topic

Discover whether your group is familiar with the idea that the Eucharist is a *memorial* of Jesus' death by asking questions like these:

- **What is it we are remembering in the Liturgy of the Eucharist?** *(The Last Supper; Jesus' dying on the cross; Jesus' Passover through death to new life.)*

- **Why do you think Catholics get together every week (or even every day) to remember Jesus' death?** *(Accept all reasonable answers.)*

Suggest to your group that in this lesson they will discover something about the importance of memory and ritual in the liturgy and in our lives as Christians.

The Scripture

Allow your group to share their thoughts on the meaning of this Scripture and its relation to the Mass.

Our Lives

Have your group read the first paragraph in this section aloud or silently. Ask them to share their experiences of memory helping us to relive and re-feel past events. Then lead them though this exercise:

Ask the group to close their eyes, relax, and become quiet. Ask them to picture in their minds a favorite place, a special memory, a good time they had, or any time when they were happy. Lead them to explore that memory with these kinds of instructions. Go slowly through each step to allow time for them to enter into the experience.

Look around in your mind's eye and see what's around you. Where are you? Who is with you?

Recall the conversations or activities that made this a happy time for you. In your mind's eye, watch it all happen again; hear the sounds. Which of your senses are most involved? How do you feel? Take a few moments to enjoy this memory.

Help your group to understand the experience with questions like this:

- **What does this experience tell us about memory?** *(Our memories allow us to relive events that already happened; past experiences can become current experiences through memory; we can have the same feelings over again by remembering.)*

Have your group read the Ritual and Memory section aloud or silently. Use questions like these to explore the story's meaning:

- **What was so important about that nativity scene?** *(Mrs. Ruiz had brought it from Mexico; it belonged to her mother; it reminded her of her home and family.)*

- **What ritual helped the family express the importance of this nativity scene?** *(They sang; the youngest child put the statue of the baby Jesus in the crib; she walked slowly and knelt down.)*

- **What memories were attached to that nativity scene?** *(Mrs. Ruiz' memories of Christmases in Mexico; her memories of her mother.)*

- **What did that ritual and those memories do for the Ruiz family?** *(It helped the children get to know their grandmother, whom they had never met; it made them a closer family; it helped them experience what family is all about.)*

Allow the group to share briefly about what rituals, Christmas or otherwise, are important in their families. What do those rituals do for your family?

Our Liturgy

Suggest to your group that as they read the next paragraph, they should look for the meaning of ritual and remembering in liturgy. Allow your group to read the first paragraph aloud or silently. Then explore the connections with questions like these:

- **How is our liturgy similar to the Ruiz family's Christmas ritual?** *(They both make memories alive again; "family" takes on new meaning for the Ruiz family; Jesus takes on new meaning for us in the liturgy.)*

- **What does our liturgical remembering do for us?** *(It brings the meaning of Jesus into our lives again; it renews our feeling for Jesus and our faith; we become part of the life of Jesus through liturgy; we enter into the paschal mystery.)*

- **What does it mean to say that we *enter into the paschal mystery* through liturgy?** *(We become like Jesus; we put on Jesus' life as though it were our own.)*

Optional Activity: Using the drawing paper and coloring medium you brought, ask each member of the group to draw a picture about entering into the paschal mystery. (They may draw something symbolic, or they may draw a situation.) Allow time for them to share the meaning of their drawings with the group. Suggest that they keep this with the pictures they drew in Lesson 4 (listening and responding) and lesson 10 (meal and sacrifice). Together, these drawings show important movements in our liturgy.

Introduce the next section by explaining that the eucharistic prayer is the central part of the ritual that helps us remember. Have your group read the next section aloud or silently. This would be a good time to incorporate the activity from the In Our Parish section.

 # Something to Know

Review the terms in this section.

 # Living Our Liturgy

Have your group read this section aloud or silently. Ask them to describe the feelings they have about trying to enter into the paschal mystery. They may express pride that Jesus has included them in his plan, or excitement about being able to come so close to God. If they express feelings of being overwhelmed or discouraged by the enormity of it all, suggest that life is full of small ways to make this a reality.

Offer examples from your own life and ask for examples from theirs. (Any situation that required some sacrifice; any situation in which someone stood by what was right in the face of pressure to back down; any situation in which we treated kindly a person we didn't really like or didn't really know.) This should set the stage for completing the next section.

 # Something to Do

Allow your group to complete this section and share their responses.

Prayer Experience

- *Option I:* Gather your group in a prayer center or in a circle. Sing "Song of the Body of Christ" by David Haas or "We Remember" by Marty Haugen.

- *Option II:* Instruct your group to repeat the response after each prayer:

Leader:	All:
When we bring the bread and bring the wine …	*Let us live in memory of you, Lord.*
When we recall your saving death …	*Let us live in memory of you, Lord.*
When we break the bread and share the cup …	*Let us live in memory of you, Lord.*

When we show compassion to those in need ...	*Let us live in memory of you, Lord.*
When we stand up for what is right ...	*Let us live in memory of you, Lord.*
When we make a sacrifice for someone else ...	*Let us live in memory of you, Lord.*
When dying and rising is part of our lives ...	*Let us live in memory of you, Lord.*

Leader: Lord Jesus, you gave us the precious gift of memory so we could know you in the liturgy. Give us now the gift of your compassion, your faithfulness, and your willingness to sacrifice, so that the liturgy may have its effect in our lives. We ask this through Christ our Lord.

Liturgy of the Eucharist: Real Presence

Objectives

- To understand that, at liturgy, the bread and wine truly become the Body and Blood of Jesus.

- To connect our celebration of the Eucharist with the need to do justice.

- To become comfortable with the options regarding reception of the Eucharist.

- To be familiar with the terms and objects used in connection with the Eucharist.

Preparation

- Read Lesson 14 and its handout in advance.

- If possible, arrange to show your group the tabernacle and the sanctuary lamp.

- If possible, arrange to have a priest or communion minister visit your group. This person could describe for the group what eucharistic ministry means to them. Such a person would also make a good "tour guide" should your group be able to visit the tabernacle and other places.

- Gather the information you need to guide your group through the In Our Parish section. Perhaps the social concerns coordinator, or similar personnel, could provide information on the areas of charity and justice in which your parish is involved.

Supplies

- Sufficient copies of Lesson 14 Handout

- Sufficient pens or pencils

- A Bible

- *Optional:* sufficient copies of the After-Mass Worksheet

Background

Belief in the real presence of Jesus in the Eucharist has been a hallmark of Catholic faith from its inception. Though disciples even in earliest times found it a difficult teaching (cf. Jn 6:60), it is nonetheless at the heart of our belief about the meaning and purpose of liturgy. Catholics take Jesus at his word. "This is my body" means exactly that. "This is my blood" means the same.

It is true that theological debate about the nature of Jesus' presence in the Eucharist has raged unrelenting through the centuries. Misunderstood and misrepresented, the Catholic faith in the real presence has led to accusations of cannibalism and cultism. This belief became a central issue in the Protestant Reformation and the Catholic counter—Reformation. Even today, it remains a "stumbling block" among Christian churches. It would, of course, be impossible, and not particularly useful, to deal with every aspect of this theology in this setting. What *is* offered in this lesson is a straightforward presentation of the church's faith. Then we look at the implications of this belief for our relationship with Jesus, our relationship with our church, and our relationship with the world.

The Catholic belief that the bread and wine *become* the Body and Blood of Jesus is completely consistent with other of our important liturgical principles. For instance, we continually hold that our work at liturgy is not simply one of historical re-enactment or spiritual theater. It is God doing for us now what God did for Jesus. We come not to see what Jesus once did but to be part of what Jesus is now doing. We remember the Last Supper not for the sake of nostalgia but so that its transforming power may again live in us. As God speaks again through the Scriptures, so God again changes bread and wine into the Body and Blood of Jesus. Understood in this way, belief in the real presence doesn't seem even the least bit odd, let alone difficult.

Beyond this, the lesson asks children to make connections between the Eucharist they celebrate and their relationships with one another. Being careful with the eucharistic species, even the last crumbs and final drops, becomes a sign of our care for the Body of Christ, especially "the least of these." Becoming one with the Body of Christ, we take upon ourselves the lot of every member. This is what it means to be *in communion with* the Body of Christ. That is why communion leads us to consider justice. It is the unquestionable result of becoming one with Christ and his Body, the church.

Introducing the Topic

Explore with your group their understanding of what they are eating and drinking in communion. Accept that misunderstandings are quite common in this area, but suggest that this lesson will help them understand just what they are being offered at communion time.

The Scripture

Allow your group to share their understanding of the opening Scripture. At the end of the lesson, return to this Scripture to see what insights they might be able to add or how they may wish to amend their original thinking.

Our Lives

Ask your group if they own or know of a special object that reminds them of someone. They might have a piece of jewelry or other memento that belonged to a grandparent, for instance. Encourage them to speak about how that object reminds them of the person. Feel free to give your own example as well.

Read the Our Lives section aloud or silently. Help them make connections with questions like these:

- **Why did Amanda give Katie her favorite bear instead of one she didn't want anymore?** *(Amanda was so attached to the bear that giving it to Katie was like giving a part of herself; her feelings for the stuffed bear were just a little bit of her feelings for Katie.)*

- **How do you think the bear will help Katie remember Amanda?** *(Because it was important to Amanda, the bear will help Katie to continue to experience their friendship, even at a distance.)*

- **How is this like Mass?** *(The stuffed bear helped Katie experience her friendship with Amanda; the bread and wine help us experience our friendship with Jesus; we can be with Jesus even though he is no longer here in person.)*

Our Liturgy

Have your group read the first two paragraphs aloud or silently. Be sure they are clear about the fact that Jesus is really present, in his humanity and divinity, in the consecrated bread and wine. Younger children may need help in understanding that this does *not* mean that the wheat-flour bread suddenly comes to consist of human tissue.

It may help to explain that even the broken bread is complete communion. Eating the consecrated bread *or* drinking the consecrated wine alone is complete communion. Jesus' presence is real and whole in every drop and particle of the consecrated elements.

Have the group finish reading the section. Check for comprehension with questions like these:

- **What does it mean to say that we *become* the Body of Christ?** *(When we share in communion, we are united with Jesus and with everyone else who shares in communion. It is a sign of our oneness. By eating and drinking together, we grow closer to Jesus and to his people. We grow together as God's family.)*

- **When you come forward for communion, how do you receive the consecrated bread? How do you drink from the cup?** *(Review the accepted procedures and the options particular to your setting. Do not give the impression that one or another of the options is preferable. Remind the group that we say a strong "Amen" after the minister says "The Body of Christ" or "The Blood of Christ.")*

- What happens to the communion that is left over? *(Consecrated wine is consumed. It is not usually kept in the tabernacle. Consecrated bread is placed in the tabernacle.)*

- Why do we place the extra consecrated bread in the tabernacle? *(Because Jesus is still present; so that the church can bring communion to people who are sick or dying. This would be a good point at which to instruct or remind your group about genuflecting in front of the tabernacle as a sign of reverence.)*

- What does the Eucharist tell us about the way we should treat each other? *(Because in communion we become the Body of Christ, the care we take with the consecrated bread and wine shows us how to take care of each other.)*

Something to Know

Review the terms in this section with your group. Emphasize those that are new to them. If circumstances permit, bring your group to visit the tabernacle, find the sanctuary lamp and sacrarium, and identify the chalice and ciborium. You might invite a priest or communion minister to be your "tour guide" and explain how the Eucharist is prepared and cared for.

Living Our Liturgy

Have your group read this section aloud or silently. Engage them in a discussion of the ways in which life needs to be more fair for more people. *(Accept all reasonable answers.)*

In Our Parish

Guide your group through this section, focusing especially on the works of charity and justice with which your parish is involved. If a parish leader in this area is available, invite him or her to speak with your group. Have your group consider those areas with which they would be able to help. Encourage individual, group, or family participation in some area of social concerns as a sign of our oneness with the Body of Christ.

Prayer Experience

Gather your group in a prayer center or in a circle. Proclaim the Emmaus Gospel passage: Luke 24:13–35.

Ask your group to pray silently in their hearts that they, too, will come to know Jesus more and more in the breaking of the bread. After some silence, conclude with:

Loving Father, through the power of your Holy Spirit, Jesus comes to us in communion. As we become one with Jesus and with each other, give us the courage to take care of all who belong to the Body of Christ. We ask this through Christ our Lord. Amen.

Liturgy of the Eucharist: Looking Forward

Objectives

- To explore the ways in which the liturgy puts us in touch with the not-yet-realized dimensions of God's kingdom.

- To help the group connect their experience of liturgy with the need to do justice.

Preparation

- Read Lesson 15 and its handout in advance.

- Be prepared to offer your own responses to the question in the In Our Parish section. Be prepared, as well, to accept responses different from your own. There's no telling what might mediate the sense of the eternal for others.

Supplies

- Sufficient copies of Lesson 15 Handout

- Sufficient Bibles

- Sufficient pens or pencils

- Drawing materials

- In Our Parish: a large piece of paper or poster board, with a marker

- *Prayer Option II:* a resource containing a musical setting of Psalm 34, or audio equipment and a recording

- *Optional:* sufficient copies of the After-Mass Worksheet

Background

The church has long held that the liturgy is not simply a "this worldly" exercise in prayer, but gives us a "foretaste of the eternal banquet." A *foretaste* means just an inkling, a glimpse, and salvation has often been spoken of in terms of a great banquet. (See, for example Isaiah 25:6–9 and Revelation 19:9). Hungry Israelites trying to coax a living out of the desert imagined God's salvation as a time of great feasting.

This imagery serves well in adding to our understanding of the liturgy. Here we have a festive meal that hints at the banquet to come. Here we have a window to the eternal. This is the eschatological nature of the liturgy.

Introducing the Topic

Ask your group to name some things that they look forward to doing. Then ask them how they act when something really special is about to happen. (Lead them to discuss how they behave in their excitement; focus on responses that indicate we may try to get a "head start" on our favorite activities. For instance, if you want to go for a dip in your pool, you might do your homework with your bathing suit on so you're as ready as possible. If you want to enjoy the fresh spring air, you might take your homework outside to do.)

Let your group know that in this lesson, they will find out how Mass is like getting a head start on God's kingdom.

The Scripture

This will be familiar to your group, but it may be so familiar that they've never given it much thought. Ask them to share what it means for God's will to be done on earth as it is in heaven. (Accept all reasonable answers.)

Discuss whether they ever get restless waiting for this to happen. (Children may not be eager for this if they believe it means "the end of the world." Assure them that what we're praying for is for there to be more "heaven" on earth while we are living. Discuss what that would be like.)

Our Lives

Have your group read this section aloud or silently. Even if this story does not reflect the school calendar in your particular area, see if they can connect with the heart of the story with questions like these:

- **What was Angelo looking forward to?** *(summer vacation)*

- **What made Angelo feel as though it were already summer?** *(His family was already having barbeques, going swimming, and planning their vacation. There was extra time to play.)*

- **What was making Angelo restless?** *(Having to be in school when summer was already started.)*

Our Liturgy

Allow your group to read this section aloud or silently. Check for comprehension with questions like this:

- **Why is our liturgy like Angelo being anxious for summer?** *(The liturgy makes us anxious for the coming of God's kingdom; we get a glimpse of heaven at Mass, just as Angelo was getting glimpses of summer. Angelo felt summer ways pulling him away from school; through liturgy, we feel God's ways pulling us away from the world's ways.)*

Because this may be new or difficult material for your group, spend some time with each of the prayer excerpts.

- **What does it mean to believe that the Eucharist is a "foretaste and promise of the paschal feast of heaven"?** *(Through the Holy Spirit, we can be "heavenly humans" right now in the way we treat others; the meal we share in the Eucharist is just a hint of the grand banquet of heaven.)*

- **What does it mean to say that "in this Eucharist, we touch the divine life you give to the world"?** *(That the liturgy is a meeting place for the human and the divine; that we get to take within ourselves the Body and Blood of the Son of God. If we become more and more like him, the world will be more divine and we will live forever with him.)*

- **What does it mean to pray that we might come to possess the life of Jesus completely in the kingdom?** *(That we can only live Jesus' way imperfectly while we're alive, but we will live it completely when we're in heaven; that when Jesus comes again, his way will be the only way.)*

Living Our Liturgy

After reading this section, be sure the group understands the comparison with Christopher Columbus. Though history has demonstrated that Columbus was not the first to discover America (only the first to let large numbers of Europeans in on the secret) and did not treat the natives here very well, the illustration works for these purposes. Try questions like these:

- **Can you think of others who could envision something they could not completely see?** *(For example: Martin Luther King, Jr.; Pope John XXIII.)*

- **What did they do because of the vision they had?** *(For example, organize voter registration in black communities; organize marches to bring attention to the vision; or, call a worldwide church council [the Second Vatican Council] even though most Catholics thought the church was fine the way it was.)*

You may want to interject the Something to Do activity before discussing what kind of behavior our vision of the kingdom fosters.

Something to Do

Provide drawing materials for your group to complete this activity. Encourage drawings that depict what life is like when people live God's way, not stereotypical images of clouds and cherubs. Some may prefer symbolic depictions of glory, light, or perfection.

In Our Parish

It may be best to allow your group to brainstorm their responses, without providing much explanation. It would be very effective to write their ideas on large paper or poster board. (Responses can be as unrelated as: incense; the way the communion minister goes over to the lady in the wheelchair to give her communion; how everyone at church spends time with that mentally challenged man who sits in the front row, even though he never makes any sense; when Father holds up the Body and Blood of Christ for us to see; the background music they play before Mass makes me think I'm in heaven; the way people bring food for the food pantry baskets. These and many other elements could be mentioned.)

Prayer Experience

- *Option I:* Conclude by praying the "Our Father."

- *Option II:* There are many musical settings of Psalm 34, and most of them are titled "Taste and See." If your assembly sings such a piece, either as a psalm or a hymn, use that song as your prayer for this lesson.

Concluding Rite

Objectives

- To understand the role of the Concluding Rite.

- To understand that liturgy does not exist for its own sake, but for the sake of our growth in the life in Christ.

- To help the group connect their experience of liturgy with the need to do justice.

Preparation

- Read Lesson 16 and its handout in advance.

- If possible, arrange for someone involved in the social concerns ministries to address your group.

- If this is not possible, become familiar with the works of charity and justice in which your parish is involved. This will help you guide your group through the In Our Parish section.

Supplies

- Sufficient copies of Lesson 16 Handout

- Sufficient pens or pencils

- A Bible

- *Optional:* sufficient copies of the After-Mass Worksheet

Background

A tongue-in-cheek case can be made that with the Concluding Rite we have reached the whole purpose of the liturgy. We come in order to leave. Our dismissal is like a commissioning to go out and live what we have heard and be whom we have received.

The liturgy is never really ended. While the hour-or-so of worship does come to an end, that's only our cue to take liturgy to the next level. Children in your group may not yet fully appreciate the growth they will be called to as they mature in faith, but you are planting the seeds that will help them understand it as it happens. For now, they can understand the analogy in it's simplest form: We take liturgy "to the next level" when we live as we have worshiped. Adults in your group (if any) may be better able so see how our experience of living the Gospel in the particular setting of our lives then brings us back to liturgy again, week after week. The constant interplay of life-and-liturgy is what keeps us moving to new levels of Christian living and new levels of Christian worship. In this way, Christian life and worship continually nourish and shape each other.

Introducing the Topic

Elicit from your group what they already know about the Concluding Rite. Use this as a starting point for Lesson 16.

The Scripture

Have a member of the group read the Scripture quotation aloud. Ask your group why they think these verses were chosen for the lesson about the end of the Mass. (Responses should focus on ideas about being sent out from Mass to let our "light shine." If they do not, suggest that the group return to the Scripture at the end of the lesson to draw their conclusions then.)

Our Lives

After reading this section, allow your group to connect with the story by briefly sharing their own experiences with electronic games that have many levels. Use questions like these:

- **Why is it good that there are different levels?** *(Once you master the easy level, you need more challenge; the game would be boring with only one or a few levels; it lets you play at whatever level you are good at; it lets you progress as you get better.)*

- **What are some of the differences between levels?** *(Each level gets a little harder; there may be more obstacles or "enemies," but also more ways for you to get around them.)*

Our Liturgy

Continue with the first paragraph of this section. Allow your group to ponder the analogy between Mass and electronic games with a question like this:

- **Why does this lesson suggest that the end of Mass is like some electronic games?** *(Because it's never really finished; when you get to what seems to be the end, there's another "level" to try. When Mass is over, the next level of living out the liturgy has just begun; every time we think we've mastered one level, God will show us another one; levels might get more complicated as we get older; we might find more obstacles in some levels, but God will always give us what we need to deal with them.)*

Have the group continue reading the remainder of the section. Check for comprehension with questions like these:

- **What are the components of the Concluding Rite?** *(The final blessing and the dismissal; these may be preceded by announcements.)*

- **Why is our liturgy often called "Mass"?** *("Mass" comes from the Latin word that means "dismissal"; our whole liturgy was named for the departure.)*

- **Why is the dismissal such an important part of the liturgy?** *(Because we're sent out to live the Jesus way; we're dismissed so we can take liturgy to the next level—the level of showing Jesus to others.)*

Living Our Liturgy

Have your group read this section. Assuming your group has been attending weekend liturgy while using this program, your discussion could focus on *their experience* of being formed and transformed by liturgy. You could also refer back to the first two lessons, in which the formative nature of liturgy was explored using pottery images. Guide the discussion with questions like these:

- **What have you heard or seen or done at liturgy that has really meant something to you?** *(Accept all reasonable responses.)*

- **How can you tell that you are being shaped and formed and transformed by liturgy?** *(Some may be able to speak about a Scripture passage that helped them think differently, or a relationship they have developed within the parish community. More likely, younger children particularly will be unable to pinpoint anything specific. Assure them that it's okay if they can't notice it. If clay were conscious, it would not necessarily see what it was becoming. But it would know that it had to stay on the wheel to fulfill its purpose. The same is true of liturgy. God works with us so gradually that we may not be able to see what's happening to us. We might be adults before we can talk about how much liturgy means to us. As long as we trust that our participation in liturgy is part of God's action in our lives, and we keep coming, we'll be able to fulfill our purpose as baptized members of Jesus' church.)*

- **Look again at the Scripture that begins the lesson. Any additional insights?**

Something to Do

Allow your group time to complete this section and to share their responses with one another.

In Our Parish

If a parishioner involved in social concerns or outreach activities is available to speak with your group, he or she could elaborate on parish activities in this area. Or it may be possible to meet such a person after Mass to discuss this. If not, use the information you have gathered to help your group see how the parish takes the real work of liturgy outside its own walls. Be sure to mention not only the "grand" projects like food pantries and homeless shelters, but the "simpler" ones like bringing communion to the sick and homebound, ministry at nursing homes, and so forth. Look especially for an area of outreach ministry in which your group could participate.

Prayer Experience

Gather your group in a prayer center, or in a circle. Lead the group in singing a Gospel acclamation appropriate to the season. Proclaim Matthew 25:31–40. Sing the Gospel acclamation again. Conclude with this prayer, or one of your own composition:

Gracious God,
you transform us through your word and sacrament
   into your own people.
Help us find new levels of service
so that Jesus will live in our hearts and in our world.
We ask this through Christ our Lord.

Sunday Celebrations in the Absence of a Priest

Objectives

- To distinguish between liturgy and Sunday celebrations in the absence of a priest.

- To discover what gifts there may be in worship services celebrated without a priest.

Preparation

- If priest-less celebrations are not common in your area, you may be tempted to omit this lesson. There is good to be found, however, in helping your group see beyond their own particular circumstances and in connecting them with the larger church. This lesson, then, can be used to help raise consciousness about parishes that must go without eucharistic liturgies. It can also help people imagine the possibilities should these circumstances ever become a reality in your parish.

- Read Lesson 17 and its handout in advance.

Supplies

- Sufficient copies of Lesson 17 Handout

- Sufficient pens or pencils

- *Optional:* sufficient copies of the After-Mass Worksheet

Background

Most Catholics are aware of the fact that there are no longer enough priests to staff all the Catholic parishes in the country. While still wishing to affirm the centrality of the Eucharist in the lives of Catholics, the church has made accommodations for communion services to take place when a priest is unavailable. Because this is a form of worship with which we still have comparatively little experience, answers to all the questions it raises are still in the making. Indeed, it is likely that we haven't even yet thought of all the questions!

This chapter is included to raise consciousness about priest-less Sunday worship. It is also intended to help Catholics discover new values and roles in this form of worship, and to help them see the hand of God continually guiding the Church even through such uncharted territory as that in which we now find ourselves.

Introducing the Topic

If your group is unfamiliar with Sunday celebrations in the absence of a priest, you may have to explain briefly why and where this is becoming more common.

The Scripture

Have a member of the group read the Scripture aloud. Engage them in a discussion of why it is important for believers to get together. (Responses could focus on the importance of supporting one another; of praying with and for others; of being and becoming the People of God.)

Our Lives

Have the group read the story aloud or silently. Explore its meaning with questions like:

- **Why was it so important to Christopher that Uncle Jack be home for Easter?** *(Christopher thought he was a lot of fun and liked the things he collected on his trips; Christopher seemed to feel that Uncle Jack's presence would "make or break" their celebration.)*

- **Why did Mom suggest that they should go anyway?** *(To celebrate Easter; to be with his cousins; to keep Aunt Eileen company.)*

Allow the group to brainstorm other situations in which one person's presence seems to make all the difference. For example:

At (when, on) _____, it just wouldn't be the same without _____.

If it has not come up spontaneously, ask them to consider the statement: "On Sunday, it just wouldn't be the same without the priest." Allow them to share their views.

Our Liturgy

Have your group read this section aloud or silently. Be sure to take your group's circumstances into account when reviewing this material. Some may be unaware that Catholics ever go without liturgy. Other will be living it every week. Consider questions like these:

- **Why is it important for Catholics to gather even when there is no priest?** *(To pray and hear the word of God; to support one another; to celebrate and strengthen their faith.)*

- **Why is a communion service not the ideal way for Catholics to celebrate on Sunday?** *(It is not the way Jesus asked to be remembered; the sacrifice of Jesus is not made present again; Eucharist can only be offered in the form of bread.)*

- **What are some things we can learn from Sunday celebration without a priest?** *(How important the assembly is; the need for lay leadership; our need to be with other believers; the fact that we are the church even without a priest.)*

If priestless Sundays are a common experience for your group, ask them to tell what they especially like about those gatherings. (Accept all reasonable answers.)

Living Our Liturgy

After reading this section, give your group time to compose prayer petitions reflecting the needs of your particular community and the needs of the church throughout the world. These might include prayers for vocations to the priesthood, prayers for those who lead your assembly, prayers for parishes that celebrate without Eucharist on Sunday, prayers for your assembly, and the like. Move directly into the Prayer Experience, or put the petitions aside until that time.

Something to Do

The chart provided with this lesson allows the group to consider the differences and similarities between a eucharistic liturgy and a Sunday celebration without a priest. Give them time to complete the chart and share their observations. Help them avoid the attitude that the two are "just about the same except we skip a couple of parts when there's no priest." What's missing when there is no priest is the re-presentation of the Last Supper and the sacrifice of Calvary.

In Our Parish

Guide your group through this section. If the second question applies to your circumstances, try having your group role-play the situation described. What did their role-play say about the church, about the assembly, and about being without a priest on Sundays?

Prayer Experience

Gather your group in a prayer center, or in a circle. Choose an appropriate response to the petitions they have prepared. Allow each member to pray his or her petition aloud, with all responding.

After-Mass Worksheet

After-Mass Worksheet

Complete this worksheet on a Saturday evening or Sunday after you've been to Mass.

What thoughts and feelings did you bring to Mass with you today? _____

_____

_____

What did I see and what did it mean?

What color vestments did I see the priest wear? _____

_____

Where else in the church did I see that color? _____

_____

When I see that color I think of _____

_____

What else did I see in church that meant something to me? _____

_____

What did I hear and what did it mean?

In the church: What were the "people sounds" before and after Mass? During Mass? _____

_____

In the music: What mood, what song(s), what instrument sounds stood out? _____

_____

In the Scriptures: The Scriptures I heard made me think _____

_____

The homily was about _____

_____

What message do I want to keep in mind and/or share with others? _____

_____

Did I speak with any other parishioners before or after Mass? With whom and about what?

_____

What did I do and what did it mean?

How did I get ready before arriving at the church? _____

_____

Did I help to build a welcoming community? How? Who else helped? _____

_____

How did I get ready after I arrived at the church? _____

_____

How did I participate in the liturgy? _____

_____

Taking liturgy to the next level

How did I experience God at liturgy today? _____

_____

What thoughts and feelings did I bring home from Mass today? _____

_____

What is this experience of liturgy calling me to do? _____

_____

Was there anything about today's experience of liturgy that got in the way of worship?

_____

_____

Catechetical Resources

THE CATECHUMENATE ANSWER BOOK
ML Answers the 101 Most-Asked Questions

Paul Turner

Paper, 160 pages, 5½" x 8½",
0-89390-501-1

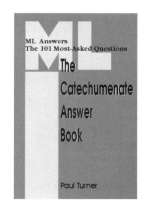

Here is a reference work that every member of your parish catechumenate team can use. Written by Ministry & Liturgy columnist Paul Turner, *The Catechumenate Answer Book* answers 101 questions that range from the basic to the historical and from the practical to the catechetical. Use this authoritative work to answer questions from catechumens, to help find solutions to pastoral dilemmas, to generate ideas for the celebration of the rites, and to make sure your catechumenal process is going in the right direction. Make sure everyone on your team has a copy.

A sampling of questions:

Why can't we do it the old way where Father did it all? Which Baptism counts? What is the difference between a sponsor and a godparent? Why do we dismiss catechumens? Should catechumens take a new name at Baptism? What is a neophyte? What does a sample catechetical session look like? Who should sign the book? How does the dismissal happen? Who leads the catechesis?

Use these stories like Jesus did to reach people on the margins ...

JESUS AND THE KINGDOM OF NOBODIES
Stories of Compassion for Faith Sharing and Homily Preparation

Andre Papineau, SDS

Paper, 136 pages, 5½" x 8½",
0-89390-514-3

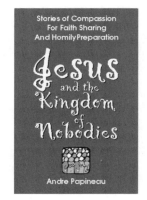

The 16 stories in this collection are especially designed to help you speak to modern outcasts — whether they feel left out because of their economic status, their age, or their pyschological state. Each story tells about individuals who either think of themselves or of others as nobodies. In the course of the story, Jesus or a Jesus figure enters the scene and accepts these nobodies as persons who belong to the new social order called God's kingdom. Each story is linked to the Roman lectionary and concludes with a helpful reflection.

Apply mystagogical thinking to every phase of the RCIA ...

CREATING AN EFFECTIVE MYSTAGOGY
A Handbook for Catechumenate Leaders

Dennis Chriszt, C.PP.S

Paper, 240 pages, 5½" x 8½",
0-89390-515-1

Catechumens may tend to think of their Baptism as a kind of graduation and cease to participate further. To confront this problem, Chriszt suggests applying "mystagogical thinking" to every step of the catechumenate process — not just the final mystagogical phase. His book provides a roadmap for doing this — from the precatechumenate, through the period of enlightenment, to the mystagogical period itself.

Guided Meditations

GUIDED MEDITATIONS FOR TEENS
Living Through the Church Year

Sydney Ann Merritt

Paper, 192 pages, 5½" x 8½",
0-89390- 402-3

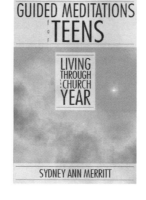

These 41 meditations, based on the church year, will guide your teenagers to a deeper relationship with Jesus. The teens will be led into a Gospel scene where they will encounter the Lord through touch, feel, love and prayer. The book is designed to primarily be a personal experience; however, questions or activities follow each meditation to help build Christian community.

GUIDED MEDITATIONS FOR CHILDREN
40 Scripts and Activities Based on the Sunday Lectionary

Sydney Ann Merritt

Paper, 192 pages, 5½" x 8½",
0-89390-336-1

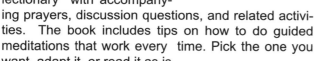

These 40 guided meditations are all related to the Sunday lectionary with accompanying prayers, discussion questions, and related activities. The book includes tips on how to do guided meditations that work every time. Pick the one you want, adapt it, or read it as is.

GUIDED MEDITATIONS FOR ADULT CATECHUMENS

Sydney Ann Merritt

Paper, 192 pages, 5½" x 8½",
0-89390-452-X

Here are meditations guaranteed to help adult catechumens grow. These meditations, organized around the major rites, let catechumens reflect on the rites and help them unpack the experience; let them feel the raging sea beneath Peter's wooden boat; hear the gentle voice of Jesus; and experience the miracles of his touch. Includes discussion questions, music suggestions and topical and scriptural indices.

Help children experience the rites with these new guided meditations ...

GUIDED MEDITATIONS FOR CHILD CATECHUMENS

Sydney Ann Merritt

Paper, 160 pages, 5½" x 8½",
0-89390-475-9

Each of these 44 meditations is connected to one or more of the catechumenal rites. You get a guided meditation script that you can use "as is" or adapt, discussion questions, and suggestions for music that will enhance the children's experience. Topical and scriptural indices make this resource useful for other occasions as well.

Parables

PERFORMING PARABLES
Religious Folk Tales, Legends, and Fables for Readers Theater

*Matthew Powell, OP
with illlustrations by
Ade Bethune*

Paper, 80 pages, 8½" x 11",
0-89390-502-X

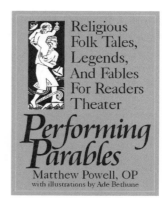

Spreading the Word is easier when you use stories and drama. And it's even easier when you have a good drama resources like *Performing Parables*. This collection of 16 religious folk tales, legends and fables is arranged in 2–15 minute readers theater segments. You don't need complicated props. You don't need much rehearsal time. You don't need to pay performance royalties. You don't even need extra books (you can photocopy the scripts you need). Just line up your talent — and an audience. These little plays, all spiced with a dash of humor, are great for prayer services, retreats, religious education classes, and parish or school functions. Includes Ade Bethune illustrations that can be used for performance programs.

PARABLES OF BELONGING
Discipleship and Commitment in Everyday Life

Lou Ruoff

Paper, 112 pages, 5½" x 8½", 0-89390-253-5

The collection of stories in *Parables of Belonging* recognizes the ability of average people to minister to others in their lives just by carrying out their day-to-day activities. Telling these stories will help listeners acknowledge and rejoice in their own "hidden" giftedness and invigorate your community.

PARABLES OF CONVERSION
Homilies and Stories Based on the Lectionary

Lou Ruoff

Paper, 128 pages, 5½" x 8½", 0-89390-403-1

"Everyone, it seems, has a favorite Father Lou homily. The one about the Lone Ranger, complete with theme song. The time he brought a sheep to the altar. The one about his buddy in Philly who tattooed his girlfriend Sue's name all over his body and ended up marrying a girl named Sharon."
—The Virginian-Pilot and the Ledger-Star.

Church Administration

HOW TO RUN A CHURCH COMMITTEE OR ORGANIZATION
A Manual for Church Leaders

Louis A. Towson

Paper, 64 pages, 8½" x 11" perforated, 0-89390-478-3

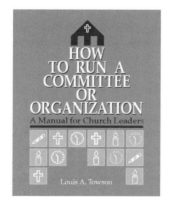

If you run a committee, this manual is indispensable. It will help you define responsibility and accountability; decide on your mission; recruit committee members; and make committee work spiritually rewarding for everyone involved. Checklists, action plans, and sample agendas help you stay on track and use committee time more productively.

THE EFFECTIVE CHURCH COMMITTEE
A Member's Handbook

Louis A. Towson

Paper, 48 pages, 5" x 7", 0-89390-479-1

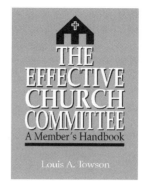

Put this booklet in the hands of every church-committee member. Committees run more smoothly when members balance assertiveness with courtesy. With an entertaining style, the author offers tips and techniques that help both newcomers and veterans become more dynamic and gracious members of the team.

MOTIVATING YOUR PARISH TO CHANGE:
Concrete Leadership Strategies for Pastors, Administrators, and Lay Leaders

Rev. Dave Heney

Paper, 128 pages, 5½" x 8½", 0-89390-433-3

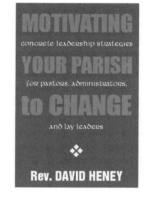

Using Moses' effort to lead his people to the Promised Land as a model, Rev. Heney lays out concrete strategies that can be applied to any parish by any person in a leadership role.

Liturgical Resources

MEANINGFUL FIRST COMMUNION LITURGIES
The Complete Planning Guide for Catechists and Teachers

Nick Wagner

Paper, 128 pages, 8.5" x 11", 0-89390-432-5

This guide, designed to accompany any First Communion prepartation program, guides you toward First Communion liturgies that are truly prayerful. Too often First Communion liturgies are planned as crowd-pleasing spectacles. This guide shows you how to plan a liturgy that is respectful while giving full attention to the three primary principles of good liturgy. This guide is not meant to replace what you're currently doing, but to supplement your current program and help it evolve. Meaningful First Communions are not just about preparing the liturgy; they're also about preparing the assembly, the families and the children for the liturgy. That's why this guide includes photocopiable preparation notes to handout to all the participants of this important ritual. You'll learn everything you need to know, from the opening procession to the recessional song.

MODERN LITURGY ANSWERS
The 101 Most-Asked Questions About Liturgy

Nick Wagner

Paper, 144 pages, 5.5" x 8.5", 0-89390-369-8

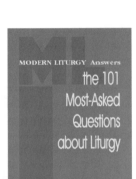

Everyone has a question about liturgy. Get answers from the editor of MINISTRY & LITURGY magazine (formerly MODERN LITURGY). You'll learn the historical and theological background of current liturgical practices — and you'll get practical solutions to vexing pastoral problems. Use this important reference book for your planning — or just to provide quick authoritative answers.

THE WORD AND EUCHARIST HANDBOOK

Lawrence J. Johnson

Paper, 168 pages, 6" x 9", 0-89390-276-4

The Word and Eucharist Handbook is your complete reference guide to liturgy. Designed for worship planners, ministers, and liturgical artists, it answers your questions about the origin, development, and modern practice of each part of the Mass.

THE LITURGICAL MUSIC ANSWER BOOK
ML Answers the 101 Most-Asked Questions

Peggy Lovrien

Paper, 160 pages, 5½" x 8½", 0-89390-454-6

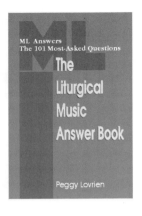

Here is a virtual training manual for music directors, song leaders, and choir members. *The Liturgical Music Answer Book* helps parish liturgical music committees study the liturgical music documents of the church, discover the appropriate ways to choose music for the liturgy, and operate with confidence in their ministry as liturgical musicians. The convenient question and answer format makes this material quickly accessible to busy liturgical musicians. From the basic, "Why do we sing at Mass?" to the practical, "What is the best way to introduce a new song?" to the specific, "Why are seat cushions bad for liturgical music?" — music committees will find satisfying answers to their nagging liturgical music questions.

More Liturgical Resources

Free trial subscription to the new MINISTRY & LITURGY magazine

Editor Nick Wagner

Ten issues per year.

If liturgy is the source and summit of parish life, it's your business — whether you are a liturgist, a religious educator, a youth minister, or a pastoral-care coordinator. That's why MODERN LITURGY (ML) has changed its name to MINISTRY & LITURGY. Check out the "new ML" for yourself. Just call us or visit our web site. You will receive the next issue of ML followed by an invoice. If you like what you see, return the invoice with a check to cover the subscription and receive the next nine issues. If you choose not to subscribe, just mark cancel on the invoice and return it. The first issue is yours to keep FREE.

Current ML subscribers: Pass on your copy of ML to a friend. Send us a copy of your ML mailing label and we'll send you a FREE replacement copy. Subscribe to ML today!